other religions
in a world of change

other religions in a world of change

william j. whalen
carl j. pfeifer, s.j.

AVE MARIA PRESS / NOTRE DAME / INDIANA 46556

Acknowledgments:
NC News Service for selected columns published originally in the
Know Your Faith summer series, © 1973
NC News Service for photos on pages 6, 22, 30, 44 and 96

Cover Photo: NASA

Nihil Obstat: The Reverend Joseph B. Collins, S.S.
              Censor Deputatus
Imprimatur: The Most Reverend William W. Baum, S.T.D.
              Archbishop of Washington

Library of Congress Catalog Card Number: 74-81341
International Standard Book Number: 0-87793-075-9

Printed in the United States of America

contents

introduction / the faiths / of other men

IF SOMEONE were to ask you to list the ten persons who have contributed most to the shaping of our world, whom would you name? Who would be your nominees for history's most influential personalities?

A respected modern historian, Arnold Toynbee, compiled such a list in response to that very question. "I would say: Confucius and Lao-tzu; the Buddha; the Prophets of Israel and Judah; Zoroaster, Jesus and Mohammed; and Socrates."

Toynbee's list of the "ten most influential persons" is made up of a handful of teachers and mystics, men of deep religious and moral convictions. Confucius and Lao-tzu were ancient Chinese sages whose teachings formed the base of Chinese culture for 25 centuries. Buddha's teachings have enlightened billions of Buddhists from India to Japan to America since he died 25 centuries ago. The prophets of Israel and Judah, men like Isaiah, Jeremiah, Hosea and Ezekiel still provide insight and inspiration to 14 million Jews as they have for some 2,500 years.

Only several hundred thousand people, chiefly the Parsis of Bombay, still follow the teachings of the Persian genius, Zoroaster (Zarathustra), but his teachings are reflected in Judaism, Islam, and Christianity.

Mohammed's teachings have helped shape the culture of countries as diverse as Pakistan, Turkey and Indonesia. As Christians we are perhaps more familiar with the profound effect the life and teachings of Jesus have had on Western civilization. Fewer of us are probably aware how greatly Jesus' teachings have been clothed in the Greek mentality and language of Socrates, and his famous pupil, Plato.

These men have had such profound and lasting influence because, among other reasons, they searched out the deepest meaning of life. They provided meaningful responses to questions each human being must face sometime during life: What is the purpose of life? What is good and evil? In what does man find happiness and fulfillment?

They shared common human experiences—joy, suffering, courage, death, moral struggle, harmony, peace —and perceived something of the mystery and depth of human life. Their insights provided hope, ideals, courage and motivation to billions of men and women of every race and color.

At some periods of the Church's history Christians have closed themselves to the riches to be found in the faiths of other men. But the more traditional attitude is one of openness to truth and wisdom wherever it is to be found. Today the Catholic Church, following the Second Vatican Council's explicit urgings, is struggling to recapture some of this openness. "Catholic" means, in fact, "open to the whole world."

After years of study Arnold Toynbee concluded: "In learning more and more to respect, reverence, admire, and love other faiths, we should be making progress in the true practice of Christianity. And the practice of the Christian virtue of charity need not prevent us from holding fast to what we believe to be the essential truths and ideals of our own Christian faith."

About This Book

IN THIS BOOK we explore some of the faiths of other men. One after another we focus on the great religions and on important dimensions of their religious tradition—not to compare or judge, but to learn. Each faith tradition challenges us to reflect more deeply on some question, experience or value in our lives. Together we may find that openness to them can actually encourage us to deepen our appreciation and understanding of our own Christian heritage, rather than being fearful of the faiths of other men.

In the first part of each chapter, William J. Whalen gives the main facts of origin, historical development, doctrinal content, and number of believers in each religion. In the second part of the chapter Carl J. Pfeifer, S.J., selects one significant aspect of each faith in an attempt to uncover something of its inner spirit.

chapter 1/the /hindus

1 *

THE RELIGION of Hinduism began to take shape more than 3,500 years ago when Aryan people invaded the Indian subcontinent and brought with them their sacred lore known as the Vedas. The various parts of the Vedas, especially the Upanishads, comprise the scriptures of this, the oldest major religion.

The word "Hindu" is simply a Persian word for the geographical region known as India. Relatively few people follow the Hindu way outside of India itself but this religion commands the allegiance of about 85 percent of those living in modern India.

Belief in reincarnation or the transmigration of souls is taken for granted in Hinduism. Each soul *(Atman)* passes through an endless series of births, deaths, and reincarnations. In Judaism, Christianity, and Islam man is born and dies only once.

Closely tied to belief in reincarnation is belief in the law of *karma*. This law of *karma* means that everyone reaps what he sows, if not in this life, then in the next. If he encounters poor health, poverty, personal tragedy in this life it is explained as the penalty for

---

* Throughout this book William J. Whalen is the author of the first part of each chapter and Carl J. Pfeifer, S.J., is the author of the second part.

evil deeds in a previous existence. According to *karma* everyone gets what he deserves.

Another aspect of Hinduism, related to both re-incarnation and *karma,* has been the caste system. Hindu society is divided into four main castes and as many as 2,000 subcastes.

Highest of the four castes is that of the Brahmans, who are the intellectuals and rulers. Then come the warriors, the merchants and farmers, and finally the workers. Even below the lowest caste are the millions of "outcastes" or untouchables. Membership in a particular caste has determined social status, choice of a marriage partner, occupation, eating habits, dress, and religious practices.

Gandhi took up the cause of the untouchables and called them *harijans* or "children of God." The new Indian constitution abolishes untouchability but discrimination has not been completely eliminated any more than it has in the United States.

Viewing Hinduism as the religion of some 450 million people, we can distinguish between the folk religion of the Indian masses and the Hinduism of the educated and sophisticated elite. The latter may see Brahman as the God above all other gods, the supreme divinity.

Brahman's chief attributes are seen through the main trinity of Brahma the creator, Vishnu the preserver, and Shiva the destroyer. Other aspects of the godhead are exemplified by literally millions of other gods. Some educated Hindus embrace a form of pantheism while others see some distinction between the individual soul and Brahman.

The average Indian peasant, however, is likely to follow a form of polytheism. Among all the gods he will choose one as his patron and cultivate devotions to this god. It might be Vishnu or Shiva or an incarnation such as Rama or Krishna or some other god.

The Hindu passes through four stages of life. The young man is initiated into the religion and receives the sacred thread; he begins his spiritual journey under the guidance of a teacher or guru. Next come the years of marriage and family, career, and community life.

In the third stage, the Hindu enters a period of detachment in which the former goals of pleasure, worldly success, and duty are left behind to pursue the goal of liberation from the limitations of life. In the fourth stage the Hindu prepares himself for passage to the next life.

To achieve the desired liberation the Hindu employs the various techniques of yoga which means "yoking of the mind to God." These techniques range from those which rely on posture and controlled breathing to those which emphasize meditation.

A member of the Brahman castes follows a daily routine of ceremonial bathing, prayers, sacrifice, and visits to the temple. Marriages are usually arranged by the parents; bride and groom may not even meet before the wedding ceremony.

Hinduism is unusually tolerant of other religious beliefs. Many Hindus such as Gandhi have expressed their admiration for Jesus and the Sermon on the Mount without acknowledging the Christian belief in his divinity.

The Fathers of the Second Vatican Council praised many aspects of Hinduism: ". . . in Hinduism men contemplate the divine mystery and express it through an unspent fruitfulness of myths and through searching philosophical inquiry. They seek release from the anguish of our condition through ascetical practices or deep meditation or a loving, trusting flight toward God."

2

Recently some friends of mine returned from a trip to India. They had taken many photographs during their travels and had put together a slide show. I spent a delightful evening with them viewing their slides and listening to their impressions of life in India.

I was struck by the number of slides which included cows wandering around freely in cities as well as rural villages. My friends had strong reactions to the cows, quite different feelings from the respect the Indians showed these animals. For the Hindus of India cows are not raised for milk or beef, but are considered sacred.

Although perhaps puzzling to tourists like my friends, the sacred cows symbolize one of the profoundest Hindu beliefs. They are a constant reminder of the sacredness of all living beings. Protection of sacred cows is to the Hindu an expression of the principle of nonviolence *(ahimsa)* based on reverence for every form of life.

The great fighter for Indian independence, Mahatma Gandhi, described the challenging Hindu ideal symbolized by the sacred cows. "Cow protection to me is infinitely more than mere protection of the cow. The cow is merely a type for all that lives.

"Cow protection means protection of the weak, the helpless, the dumb, and the deaf. Man becomes then not the lord and master of all creation but he is its servant. The cow to me is a sermon on pity."

The Hindu ideal of reverence for all life is translated into nonviolent actions as diverse as abstaining from meat (lest an animal be killed) and the nonviolent strategies of civil disobedience designed by Gandhi. The profound Hindu motivation for reverence receives a variety of interpretations, depending on the theological sophistication of the individual Hindu.

For some Hindus reverence for life borders on superstition or is accepted merely as a traditional practice of Indian culture. For others Brahman is a personal God who lives in all that has life.

Whatever the variety of theological interpretations of Hindu reverence for life, Hindu tradition recognizes life as sacred, as mysterious. For Hindus like Gandhi, reverence for life, symbolized by the sacred cows, is a central expression of Hindu faith.

Nourished on the most popular of Hindu scriptures, the *Bhagavad-Gita,* Gandhi and billions of Hindus have accepted as a guiding principle the words of Krishna in the *Gita:* "A man should not hate any living creature. Let him be friendly and compassionate to all."

While cow protection may seem very strange and foreign to the average steak-loving American, the deep Hindu ideal it symbolizes presents us with challenging food for thought regarding our own attitudes toward life, and our Christian tradition of respect for life. Hindu reverence for life, mediated through the example and writings of Gandhi, profoundly influenced nonviolent strategies in recent American history, particularly as advocated by Martin Luther King, Jr.

The Hindu ideal of reverence symbolized by sacred cows may stimulate us to probe more deeply into our own Christian tradition as we grapple with the challenges of our times. Many vital issues of contemporary life revolve around one's reverence or lack of reverence for life: abortion, mercy killing, medical experimentation, pollution, civil disobedience, capital punishment, war and indiscriminate bombing.

QUESTIONS

1. T. or F.—The various parts of the Vedas, especially the Upanishads, comprise the scriptures of the Hindu religion.

2. In the Hindu religion, belief in reincarnation is closely tied to the law of ...., which means that everyone reaps what he sows, if not in this life then in the next.

3. The .... system is another aspect of Hinduism, and is related to both reincarnation and the law of *karma*.

4. In India, the .... is considered a sacred animal.

5. T. or F.—The Hindu religion stresses the principle of nonviolence based on a great reverence for all forms of life.

6. .... was a great fighter for Indian independence, and a follower of the Hindu religion.

chapter 2/the
/buddhists

1

IN THE SIXTH CENTURY before Christ the founder of
a new sect within Hinduism proposed a method of
liberation which even the lower castes could follow.
Eventually this sect was branded as heretical and became a religion separate from Hinduism. It is known
as Buddhism.

The founder of Buddhism was born into the war-
rior caste in India about 560 B.C. As a young man
Siddhartha Gautama was apparently shielded from the
harsher realities of life such as death, disease, and
poverty.

Gautama married and had one son. But when he
faced the fact of pain and suffering he found no satis-
faction in the answers given by Hinduism. He left his
family to begin a search for a better solution to the
problem of suffering.

Gautama continued his spiritual search for five or
six years. Yoga, fasting, meditation, mortification failed
to show the way. Finally while sitting under a bo tree
he experienced the illumination which revealed the
true path to emancipation. From then on he was
known as the Buddha or the Enlightened One.

Buddha proclaimed the Four Noble Truths. First,
that existence involves suffering. Second, that suffering

is caused by desire. Third, that the way to escape suffering is to eliminate desire. And fourth, that to quench desire a man should follow the Eightfold Path.

This Eightfold Path prescribed by Buddha asks that a man pursue right thoughts, right intentions, right speech, right action, right livelihood, right effort, right mindfulness, and right concentration.

Buddha and his followers adopted an agnostic position regarding the existence of God and other metaphysical questions. Buddhism concentrates on how a man can extinguish the three main desires which lead to suffering: the desires for pleasure, prosperity, and continued existence. The effort to extinguish these desires may take more than one lifetime but Buddhism holds out the hope that man can in time achieve the desired liberation or *nirvana*.

— At first Buddha imparted his teaching to a group of monks but as time passed Buddhism spread to the masses in India and other Asian countries. Buddha spent nearly 45 years preaching and counseling but he never wrote down his teachings. About 150 years passed before this oral teaching was committed to writing.

Buddhism has had a major influence on every Oriental culture although it no longer has many adherents in its homeland in India. The estimated 300 million Buddhists belong to various sects.

— The form known as Mahayana or the Greater Vehicle predominates in China, Japan, Korea and Viet Nam. One of the distinctive features of this school is the belief in Bodhisattvas. Something like "saints," the Bodhisattvas are beings which have qualified for *nirvana* but out of compassion for mankind have postponed their reward in order to help men achieve the same goal. They visit the earth in incarnations to help people follow the true way.

Hinayana or the Lesser Vehicle is the form of Buddhism found in Thailand, Ceylon, Burma, Cambodia, Laos and Indonesia. Its adherents prefer the term "Theravada" and claim to be closer to the original ideas of Buddha. In Tibet, Buddhism combined with magic and demon worship in what we know as Lamaism. Perhaps 100,000 Americans, mostly of Japanese ancestry, practice Buddhism.

The Fathers of Vatican II observed: "Buddhism in its multiple forms acknowledges the radical insufficiency of this shifting world. It teaches a path by which men, in a devout and confident spirit, can either reach a state of absolute freedom or attain supreme enlightenment by their own efforts or by higher assistance."

Monasticism has always played an important role in Buddhism. A novice shaves his head, dons a yellow or orange robe, takes a new name, and begins to live by the 220 rules of the order.

Strictly speaking, the monks are supposed to beg for their living. Older men often enter a monastery after they have married and raised a family. Buddhist nuns follow a similar way of life. The total number of Buddhist monks and nuns is estimated at 800,000.

A form of Japanese Buddhism called Zen Buddhism has won a following among Western intellectuals and hippies. Students study the 1,700 traditional questions or *koans* such as the famous *koan,* "Tell me the sound of one hand clapping." Zen monks may meditate as long as six hours a day in their search for liberation. For some Westerners Zen is more of a philosophy or intellectual technique than a religion.

2

Slowly I paged through a book of remarkably sensitive photographs by the late *Life* photographer, Larry Burrows. There was a pensive little girl waiting to be fitted with an artificial leg, a widow weeping over the body of her husband, and tear-filled faces of young and old. There was a beggar dying in a Calcutta train station, a person undergoing surgery in a remote region of Burma, and a tough GI weeping after a buddy's death.

The book called up all the suffering of mankind. Its title revealed the heart of the photographer: *Larry Burrows—Compassionate Photographer.*

As I studied his photos of suffering persons, my mind wandered back some 25 centuries to the fascinating story of Siddhartha Gautama, known to the world as Buddha. Brought up in luxury by an overprotective father, Siddhartha knew only young, beautiful, healthy people during his entire youth.

Then one day as he rode happily along in his chariot, he came upon an old man hobbling along the road with a crutch. Shortly after, he met a sickly man, his face wracked with pain. Then he encountered a funeral procession.

Never before had he known suffering. His sensitive heart was deeply troubled. The sight of a peaceful monk walking along the road intensified his anguish. How could one find peace in a world marred by such pain?

In his struggle to make sense out of life's sorrows he left his luxurious home. After six years of searching, he experienced a memorable night of enlightenment. The next morning he formulated what was to become the basis of faith for billions of men and women down to the present day.

"Life," he said, "is suffering!" "Suffering," he went on, "arises out of selfish craving for pleasure, power and continued life." He continued: "Suffering ceases with the cessation of these selfish desires." To these three insights he added a practical eightfold path for stifling selfish craving. Known as the Four Noble Truths these insights into life's meaning provide the foundation of Buddhist faith.

Enlightened by this knowledge, Buddha was moved by compassion for suffering mankind. Instead of continuing to enjoy the happy state of *nirvana* he achieved during the night of his enlightenment, he traveled up and down India teaching his Four Noble Truths and Eightfold Path of Righteousness. He devoted the remaining 45 years of his life to sharing his saving knowledge with those caught up in the mystery of life's sorrows. Countless millions of men and women for 2,500 years have therefore revered him as the "compassionate Buddha."

While the several branches of Buddhism reveal a wide variety of theological interpretations, religious practices, and life-styles, all embrace as an ideal the compassion of Buddha. Entitled to the enjoyment of *nirvana,* he freely postponed that enjoyment to spend himself on behalf of suffering mankind.

Buddhists recall the saying of Buddha about the primacy of love: "None of the means employed to acquire religious merit, O monks, has a sixteenth part of the value of loving-kindness. Loving-kindness, which is freedom of heart, absorbs them all."

The way to overcome the selfishness that is the cause of human suffering is that of compassionate love. Unselfish love brings freedom from selfish desire.

His faithful followers, never forgetting Buddha's example and teaching of compassion, seriously struggle to overcome selfishness by growing in compassion.

Whether they revere Buddha as a great teacher or worship him as divine, he remains the compassionate Buddha. His way is one of compassionate and universal love.

Larry Burrows' photos remind one of the pervasiveness of suffering in man's life. Buddha has provided insight into human suffering and a way of coping with it for literally billions of people during 25 centuries. As we grow in understanding and admiration of Buddhist ideals, we do well to reflect on the richness of our Christian insights into suffering and ask ourselves how well we live up to the challenge of Jesus: "Be compassionate as your heavenly Father is compassionate" (Lk 6:36).

QUESTIONS

1. T. or F.—The religion of Buddhism was originally a part of the Hindu religion, becoming a separate religion in the sixth century before Christ.

2. The founder of the Buddhist religion was . . . .

3. T. or F.—Monasticism has no relationship at all to the religion of Buddha.

4. Gautama said that "life is . . . . , which rises out of selfish craving for pleasure, power and continued life."

5. T. or F.—The founder of the Buddhist religion was always a poor man.

6. The way of Buddha is one of compassionate and universal . . . .

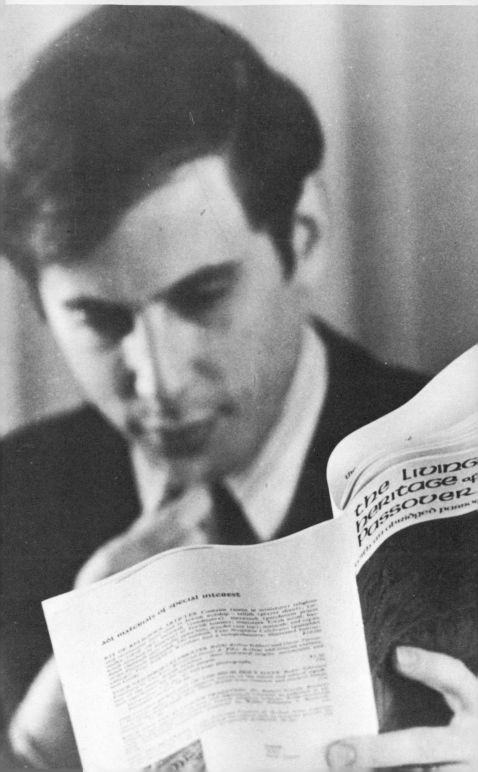

chapter 3/the /jews

1

FROM ONE SMALL nomadic tribe have come three major religions which claim the allegiance of almost half the world's population. This people's God named Yahweh and their moral code called the Ten Commandments have also become the God and code of Christianity and Islam. The descendants of this Middle Eastern tribe are known as Jews and their religion is Judaism.

Men and women of Jewish heritage have contributed so enormously to Western civilization that we can hardly imagine what life would be like without them. An itinerant preacher known as Jesus founded a religious faith which more than 900 million people profess. A Viennese physician, Sigmund Freud, revolutionized man's understanding of himself.

Karl Marx gave birth to the political philosophy which now rules Soviet Russia, China, and a dozen other nations. Albert Einstein, a mathematical genius, developed the theories which led to the dawn of the atomic age. Out of all proportion to their numbers Jews have become scientists, musicians, scholars, writers, financiers, and teachers.

Despite centuries of persecution, culminating in the massacre of six million Jews by the Nazis, an estimated 14 million people identify themselves as Jews. Almost half of these now live in the United States but for the first time in 2,000 years the Jews control their own state, Israel.

Jews, Christians and Moslems honor an ancient tribal figure called Abraham as the patriarch of the Jewish people along with Isaac and Jacob. What set Abraham apart from the other tribal leaders some 4,000 years ago was his belief that there was only one God.

Eventually the tribe of Abraham was enslaved by the Egyptians but they were led to freedom by another remarkable leader, Moses. On behalf of his people Moses entered into a covenant with Yahweh. They would worship only him and observe his commandments and he would protect them as his special people. Around the year 1200 B.C. these people settled in the fertile land of Canaan.

As a relatively small tribe they were usually threatened by their stronger neighbors. In 721 B.C. the northern kingdom of Israel went into exile in Assyria and in 587 B.C. the southern kingdom of Judah fell to the Babylonians.

When the Persians conquered the Babylonians in 539 B.C. they allowed a remnant of Jews to return to their homeland. Still they would live under the rule of others: Persians, Greeks, Syrians. In 63 B.C. the Romans assumed control and in 70 A.D. Roman armies put down a rebellion, destroyed the temple, killed, enslaved and dispersed the Jews.

Without a homeland of their own the Jews would settle in Russia, Poland, Germany, England, France, Latin America, the U.S., Canada and even in India and China. They carried with them their scriptures, the collection of sacred writings begun during the reign of King David and continued for 1,000 years. They called the first five books of the bible the Torah, or law; the numerous later commentaries were known as the Talmud. The Jews of the diaspora were sustained through history by their ethical standards, their dietary laws and ritual, their simple creed: "Hear, O Israel, the Lord our God, the Lord is One."

The Jews had looked forward to one who would come to redress all wrongs and restore Israel's former glory. He would be the Messiah sent to the chosen people by Yahweh. Those who accepted Jesus as the promised Messiah were originally all Jews but the message of the gospel was to be proclaimed to the Gentiles as well as the Jews.

Until the destruction of the temple in 70 A.D. the chief form of Jewish worship was sacrifice. Now it is prayer and meditation and reading of the scriptures. Rabbis (teachers) furnish spiritual leadership to the congregations.

Stressing Christianity's ties with Judaism, the Fathers of the Second Vatican Council declared: "The Church repudiates all persecutions against any man. Moreover, mindful of their common patrimony with the Jews, and motivated by the gospel's spiritual love and by no political considerations, she deplores the hatred, persecutions, and displays of anti-Semitism directed against the Jews at any time and from any sources."

2

"From my favorite spot on the floor I look up at the blue sky and the bare chestnut tree, on whose branches little raindrops shine, appearing like silver, and at the seagulls and the other birds as they glide on the wind. . . . As long as this exists, and I may live to see it, this sunshine, the cloudless skies, while this lasts, I cannot be unhappy."

So wrote 14-year-old Anne Frank from her hiding place in Amsterdam in February 1944. A year later, in March 1945, she died in the Belsen concentration camp.

Anne was a Jew. She shared the pain and persecution so many of her fellow Jews have endured during some 30 centuries. She exemplified the quiet joy that seems to characterize the faith of Jews in times of peace and pain from the days of Abraham, Moses and David, to the present. Joy and a sense of humor seem to typify Jewish faith even during the blackest hours.

The joy of Jews is typically rooted in the earth, in the good things of life, because their God creates all that is and takes an active part in their experience. A famous Jewish writer, Elie Weisel, wrote: "To be a Jew is to opt for God and creation alike—it is a refusal to oppose one to the other."

From Babylon to Belsen faithful Jews have preserved their faith in the goodness of man and the world as they kept faith with God. They appear to have done so with a smile, reflecting an enduring inner peace and joy.

Jews believe that while God utterly transcends this world, he is intimately involved in each phenomenon of nature and every human experience. Although Jews respect God's awesome holiness to such an extent that they do not even utter his name, they know that he delights in the company of people. They praise him for "producing bread from the earth and wine to gladden men's hearts" (Ps 104:15).

The major Jewish festivals to this day combine the enjoyment of life's good things with the joy of knowing God's presence. The festival of Passover *(Pesach)* celebrates the freeing presence of God today as in the days of Moses, and at the Seder meal the father reminds his family, "He brought us from slavery to freedom. . . . Let us then sing a new song in his presence. Hallelujah!"

The Feast of Weeks *(Shavuoth)*, 50 days after Passover, celebrates the enduring covenant between God and his people. This bond is as enduring as the sun and moon, as unshakable as the mountains, as intimate and tender as marital love.

Autumn brings the joyful festival of Booths *(Sukkot)*. Amidst temporary shelters made of branches and leaves Jewish communities eat and drink in happy remembrance of the days when their fathers knew God's presence as they wandered in the desert. Believing God is with them today as then, they thankfully enjoy the good things of earth which in so many ways reveal his presence.

The Sabbath provides a weekly opportunity for the Jewish family to enjoy life's blessings and deepen their faith in the creator of all. As the Sabbath draws to a close the Jewish family prays: "Sovereign of the universe, Father of mercy and forgiveness . . . cause us to hear in the coming week tidings of joy and gladness. . . . Bless and prosper the work of our hands."

The faith of Jews, marked even in the midst of persecution and suffering by joy and appreciation of the good things of life, can be a stimulus for us Christians to look at our own faith. How closely is our faith in God related to the ordinary realities of daily living? How genuinely do we appreciate the world in which we live, seeing it as a sign of God's presence and love? How truly does our faith in God overflow into that joy Jesus came to deepen in us? (Jn 15:11).

QUESTIONS

1. T. or F.—Jews, Christians and Moslems all honor Abraham as the patriarch of the Jewish people.

2. The Jews call the first five books of the bible the
. . . .

3. . . . . led the Jews out of their enslavement in Egypt: a) John   b) Moses   c) Paul.

4. The joy of Jews is typically rooted in the . . . . , in the good things in life.

5. T. or F.—Jews believe that while God transcends this world, he is intimately involved in each phenomenon of nature.

6. The . . . . of Jews, marked even in the midst of persecution and suffering by joy and appreciation of the good things of life, can be a stimulus for Christians as well.

chapter 4/the
/muslims

1

MORE THAN 450 million people, mostly Asians and Africans, consider an Arab religious genius called Mohammed to be God's last and greatest prophet. They consider the book he dictated, the Koran, to be his final revelation to mankind. They follow the religion of Islam which is an Arabic word which means "to submit" to the will of God (Allah).

In 7th century Arabia the founder of this religion, an unschooled camel driver, challenged the barbarism and polytheism of society by proclaiming that there is only one God (Allah) and that he is his prophet. Mohammed reported that the Archangel Gabriel had appeared to him and revealed the first part of the Koran; such visions would continue over a period of 23 years.

Familiar with Judaism and Christianity, Mohammed acknowledged that Noah, Abraham, Moses, and Jesus were also prophets sent by Allah but he denied the Christian belief in the Incarnation and the Trinity. Muslims honor Mohammed as the Seal of the Prophets but not as God.

Mohammed won few converts in his hometown of Mecca and, in fact, annoyed the local merchants who profited by the visits of pilgrims to the town's 360 pagan shrines. Opposition stiffened and in A.D. 622

Mohammed fled to the city of Yathrib (renamed Medina) about 200 miles to the north. Here he was welcomed and accepted by most of the inhabitants as a spiritual and political leader. Eight years after his flight to Medina he led his forces in triumph back to Mecca. By the time of his death in 632 most of Arabia had embraced the religion of Islam.

Within 100 years the Muslims had conquered Persia, Egypt, Syria, Palestine, Iraq, and Spain. The flourishing Christian communities of North Africa and the Middle East were practically wiped out. Victorious Muslim armies crossed the Pyrenees into France but were defeated by Charles Martel at the battle of Tours in 732. Had the battle gone otherwise all of Europe and the West might be Muslim today.

The religious structure of this religion rests on the Five Pillars of Islam: creed, prayer, almsgiving, fasting, and pilgrimage. The creed consists of a single sentence: "There is no God but Allah, and Mohammed is his prophet."

Muslims are expected to pray five times a day—upon arising and at noon, midafternoon, sunset, and retiring. They also gather at noon Friday for prayers and reading of the Koran at a mosque. Islam has no sacraments, priests, images or required ritual.

The fortunate must help the less fortunate. Mohammed prescribed that each follower distribute to the poor two and a half percent of his income and property each year.

During the 30 days of the month of Ramadan every Muslim must fast from sunrise to sunset. During these daylight hours no food or drink may pass his lips.

Finally, the devout Muslim will arrange to make a pilgrimage to Mecca once during his lifetime. Islam also asks that adherents abstain from gambling, alcohol, and pork but not all Muslims observe these last two prohibitions. Those who persevere in the way of Islam are promised an afterlife of delights while the wicked will suffer in a hell of heat, scalding water, and burning desert winds.

Against the sexual promiscuity and unrestrained polygamy of his day Mohammed taught a moral code which limited a man to no more than four wives at one time. Traditionally Muslim women have lived in seclusion and were heavily veiled. Such customs are still observed in countries such as Pakistan but ignored in others such as Turkey.

Youngest of the major world religions, Islam has become the dominant religion of the Arab nations, Pakistan, Indonesia, and dozens of other African and Asian countries. Some 20 million are Soviet citizens. Islam's uncomplicated theology, easy initiation, acceptance of local customs such as polygamy, and freedom from the colonial stigma have given this religion an edge over Christian missionaries in many pagan areas.

Islam accepts Jesus as a messenger of Allah but not the Messiah or the Son of God. The Koran mentions Mary as the Mother of Jesus 34 times and teaches that only she and her mother Anne have escaped the touch of Satan.

Historically, relations between Muslims and Christians have been strained by such events as the Holy Wars against the Christians of North Africa and the Crusades which sought to free the Holy Lands from Muslim occupiers. Yet the Fathers of the Second Vatican Council affirmed that the Catholic Church views the Muslims with esteem.

The Declaration on the Relationship of the Church to Non-Christian Religions states that Muslims "adore one God, living and enduring, merciful and all-powerful" and that they "strive to submit wholeheartedly even to his inscrutable decrees, just as did Abraham. . . ." The Fathers of the Council urged both Christians and Muslims to "forget the past and to strive sincerely for mutual understanding."

2

I recently visited the beautiful Mosque in Washington, D.C., with my parents. We removed our shoes and stepped onto the rich carpets covering the entire floor. As we admired the intricate geometric designs and painted tiles, we were all struck by the atmosphere of peaceful reverence we experienced.

A Muslim guide invited us to sit on the carpeted floor as he explained to us various aspects of Islamic religious practices. While he was talking two young Muslim men walked directly to the center of the Mosque. They stood facing the niche in the wall that indicates the direction of Mecca. Precisely at noon one of the men called all followers of Mohammed to prayer, melodiously chanting the customary call in Arabic.

Our guide politely excused himself, promising to return as soon as he had completed his prayers. As we watched in silent admiration, the three carried out the prescribed ritual gestures as they recited verses from the Koran. Gracefully they followed a precise discipline—standing, kneeling, bowing down until their heads touched the carpet. After about five minutes of unembarrassed public prayer our guide rejoined us.

My parents and I were deeply impressed as we witnessed the Muslim's public expression of faith in God. Their example brought to life what I had read in books, and doubled my admiration for the courage that seems so central to the faith of Islam. To be a faithful Muslim required the courage of one's convictions, the public witness to one's faith.

Mohammed himself exemplified such moral courage. He spoke out publicly against the intrigue and injustice in wealthy Mecca. In spite of ridicule and threats, he condemned idolatry and proclaimed that there is only one true God, Allah. Escaping an attempted assassination, he struggled against opposition for more than eight years before winning a foothold in Mecca for his faith.

Like Mohammed, faithful Muslims today as in the past give public expression to their faith. Five times a day they perform public acts of prayer such as we witnessed in the Mosque. Significantly, the central formulation of Muslim belief is called, not a creed, but a witness: "I bear witness that there is no god but Allah, and that Mohammed is his prophet." Faithful Muslims are called to courageously witness to that faith even if it involves the risk of death.

Islam is to me a powerful reminder of the importance of moral courage, the willingness to take a public stand for one's convictions and principles. Public commitment to God and moral principles is needed in a world of shifting values and rapid change. Faith demands witness. Believers need to show by moral courage in witnessing to their faith that there is Someone greater than man in this world—Someone whose power is equaled only by his love.

As I watched the Muslims pray publicly in the Mosque, I was reminded of Jesus' words to his followers—words which might cause each of us to reflect on his own life: "You will receive power when the Holy Spirit comes down on you; then you are to be my witnesses . . . even to the ends of the earth" (Acts 1:8). How real is our witness? Do we have the courage of our convictions?

QUESTIONS

1. T. or F.—"Islam" is an Arabic word which means "to submit" to the will of God (Allah).

2. The founder of the Islam religion in the seventh century was an unschooled camel driver by the name of ....

3. The religious structure of the Islam religion rests on the Five Pillars of Islam: creed, prayer, almsgiving, fasting and ....

4. In the Islamic religion, the .... is the official book of the faith.

5. T. or F.—The central formulation of Muslim belief is really not a "creed" but a "witness."

6. The religion of Islam is a powerful reminder of the importance of .... courage, the willingness to take a public stand for one's convictions and principles.

chapter 5 / the eastern / orthodox

1

FOR MORE THAN 900 years the Roman Catholic Church in the West and the Orthodox Churches in the East have gone their separate ways. After several schisms the final break came in 1054 when the pope and the patriarch of Constantinople excommunicated each other.

Attempts to heal the break were made during the Middle Ages but these failed for lack of grass-roots support. Now at long last the prospects for a reunion of the Churches of the East and West appear brighter than they have for centuries. In 1965 Pope Paul VI and Patriarch Athenagoras, spiritual leader of some 130 million Orthodox, lifted the mutual excommunications.

Catholics and Orthodox recite the same creeds and share the central Christian beliefs. Each recognizes that both Catholic and Orthodox bishops stand in the apostolic succession and ordain true priests. No one questions the validity of the seven sacraments, the nature of the Mass of the Divine Liturgy, or the honor due the Blessed Virgin Mary and the saints.

The chief difference concerns the role of the bishop of Rome, the pope, in the universal Church. The Orthodox have not accepted the understanding of the pope's jurisdiction and infallibility held by Roman Catholics; they would not withhold the title of patriarch of the West. Orthodox and Catholics also disagree on such questions as purgatory, the theological definitions of the immaculate conception, and certain subtle doctrinal matters.

Christianity began at the eastern end of the Mediterranean. The New Testament was written in Greek and the early Church Fathers and missionaries used the Greek language. All of the great councils—Nicaea, Ephesus, Chalcedon, Constantinople—were held in the East. Great Christian centers flourished in the East when Catholics had to hide in the Roman catacombs.

As the centuries passed the Christians of the East looked to the capital in Constantinople for religious leadership while those in the West gave allegiance to the bishop of Rome. One group used Greek in its worship and theological writing, the other, Latin.

Language, cultural differences, and distance drew the two sections apart. The last ecumenical council to include bishops from East and West was held in 787 A.D. Relations after the 11th-century schism were further strained by the actions of the Crusaders who sacked Constantinople in 1204.

Those churches which derive from the churches of the East are known as "Orthodox" which signifies "right belief." Sometimes they are also called Eastern Orthodox or Greek Orthodox. They believe that the Orthodox Church is the "authentic and infallible interpreter of the faith."

The commonwealth of Orthodox Churches consists of a number of independent churches who recognize the patriarch of Constantinople as the titular head of Orthodoxy. The patriarch wields no direct authority over other patriarchs or bishops; his patriarchy as such includes only a small flock in Turkey. Only about one million Orthodox fall under the direct jurisdiction of the patriarch of Constantinople and the other three ancient patriarchates of Alexandria, Antioch, and Jerusalem.

The strength of Orthodoxy lies in the independent churches of Russia, Rumania, Yugoslavia, Greece, and Bulgaria along with a number of smaller national churches. Perhaps 40 million Soviet citizens consider themselves Russian Orthodox. Most Orthodox live under Communist regimes and have borne the brunt of antireligious persecutions.

The Orthodox differ from Catholics in some customs as well as in doctrines. For example, most Orthodox parish priests are married men while bishops are drawn from the ranks of the celibate monks. Baptism is by immersion and infants are confirmed immediately after baptism. The Orthodox allow divorce for specific causes such as adultery, impotence, desertion, insanity; the innocent party may remarry.

Ecumenists pray that the relatively minor differences which keep Orthodox and Catholics apart may be resolved and the tragic division may become a thing of the past.

2

When I think of Eastern Orthodox Churches I spontaneously think not of doctrines but of worship, not of words but of symbols. I think of ikons and incense, of long, solemn liturgical services. I imagine bearded priests, wearing stiff, heavy vestments, solemnly swinging incense boats, singing liturgical chants.

Eastern Orthodox worship suggests to me a sense of awesome mystery. While much of the liturgy is visible to all, parts are carried out in secret behind a heavily curtained grille. The words that seem to recur most frequently are "Lord," and "holy." A kind of solemn wonder characterizes Eastern Orthodox worship. They even call their sacraments, "mysteries."

While I do not feel particularly at home at such lengthy, solemn liturgies—perhaps because the language and symbolism seem foreign—I find the Eastern Orthodox tradition of solemn worship most valuable. Our age is often described as becoming more and more secularized. There seems to be little sense of the sacred as science progressively probes the mysteries of nature and man, and as technology steadily increases man's control of natural powers. In contemporary culture everything seems out in the open, nothing is sacred, little remains hidden. Man's sense of mystery is in danger of dying.

Western expressions of Christianity seem to move with the secularization of today's world. Recent religious interest centers more on man than on God. Becoming more human and building a better world are recognized as ways of fulfilling the Christian ideal. Worship has tended to take the same direction, seeking to make the liturgy readily understandable and easily accessible.

While the contemporary Christian focus on man and the world is basically sound and healthy, there is a growing risk of losing the sense of mystery that is so much a part of Christian tradition. The Eastern Churches remind us that God, who is certainly with us in our world, is totally *other* than we conceive him, utterly beyond man's understanding or control. They highlight the mystery of God.

It is a common tendency to try to bring God down to human terms, to make him in the image of current human ideals and values. It is perhaps a particularly

Western temptation to think one can know God by defining him in precise words.

The Eastern Orthodox Churches preserve the Judaeo-Christian tradition of awe and wonder in the mysterious Presence of the Almighty. They are a constant reminder that man approaches God with fear and trembling, even as one approaches him confidently as a Father. They show us that worshiping God is more radically Christian than thinking, talking about and attempting to define God.

QUESTIONS

1. T. or F.—The final break between the Roman Catholic and Eastern Orthodox churches came in 1054.

2. The Eastern Orthodox Church does not accept the infallibility of the . . . .

3. The Council of . . . . was held in the East.
   a) Nicaea   b) Ephesus   c) Chalcedon   d) all of these

4. T. or F.—The Eastern Orthodox churches preserve the Judaeo-Christian tradition of awe and wonder in the mysterious presence of the Almighty.

5. The Eastern Orthodox churches call the sacraments, ". . . . ."

6. T. or F.—In the liturgy of the Eastern Orthodox churches, the words "Lord" and "Holy" seldom are mentioned.

chapter 6 / the lutherans

1

THE LUTHERAN COMMUNION is not only the oldest Protestant denomination but is also the largest on a worldwide basis. Seventy-five million Lutherans are concentrated in Germany, the Scandinavian countries of Sweden, Norway, Denmark and Finland, Brazil, Argentina and the United States.

Except for small movements, the unity of Western Christendom remained more or less intact until the start of the 16th century. Then this unity was broken by a German Augustinian friar, Martin Luther, who challenged the exercise and claims of papal authority and the condition of Church life at the time.

Luther left the study of law after a frightening experience in a thunderstorm in which he vowed to enter a monastery. Two years after joining the Augustinian order he was ordained a priest and in 1512 he received a doctorate in scripture. He was assigned to teach at the new University of Wittenberg.

At this stage of his life Martin Luther was preoccupied with the question: "What must I do to be saved?" He found no sure answers in his prayers, penances, fasting and faithful adherence to the rules of his order. But while reading St. Paul's Epistle to the Romans he was struck by the passage, "The just man lives by faith" (Rom 1:17). This would be the cornerstone of his religious system.

Along with specific criticisms of abuses in the Church he proposed the main elements of his theology in his famous 95 theses. According to the custom of his time he nailed a list of theses or propositions to be debated on the church door at Wittenberg on October 31, 1517.

He had no intention of disrupting the unity of the Church by his act but as the years passed basic differences grew. Luther was excommunicated in 1521. By the time he died in 1546 the churches of the Reformation and the Roman Catholic Church were separate bodies.

The Catholic Church in Luther's day was vulnerable to attack. Some bishops, priests, religious and laity lived saintly lives but others were corrupt. The popes often acted more like warlords or feudal kings than spiritual fathers. Poor philosophy and theology produced a folk religion which promised forgiveness of sins and attainment of salvation through purchased indulgences and "bargains" with God.

Lutheranism rests on two fundamental principles: man is restored to friendship with God by faith in Jesus Christ alone, and the bible is the only source and guide of faith and life.

Luther rejected the authority claimed by the pope and the necessity of having bishops; he reduced the role of tradition in comparison with the bible, and regarded only Baptism and Holy Communion as sacraments clearly authorized by Sacred Scripture. Worship was conducted in the vernacular instead of Latin, clergymen were allowed to marry, and the laity received both bread and wine in Holy Communion.

In retrospect Luther can be viewed as a conservative reformer. He was repelled by the extreme positions of the Anabaptists who denied the validity of infant baptism. He argued with the Calvinists over such questions as predestination and the Real Presence in the Eucharist.

In Germany, Lutherans eventually outnumbered the Catholics while in the Scandinavian countries the establishment of state Lutheran churches practically wiped out Catholic influence. The first Lutheran immigrants came to America in the 17th century and were the forerunners of the nearly nine million U.S. Lutherans. Among Protestant denominations in the United States Lutherans rank after Baptists and Methodists.

Once bitterly hostile, the Roman Catholics and Lutherans in this country and in Germany are probably friendlier now than at any time during the 450-year separation. Basic doctrinal disagreements still exist but the gulf has narrowed through theological dialogue and efforts to erase misunderstanding.

2

"Man, God is not angry with you. You are angry with God. Don't you know that God commands you to hope?"

The words have a contemporary ring. Actually they were spoken by a wise old priest to an anxious young man some 450 years ago. The young man's name was Martin Luther.

Like many a young person today, Luther was torn with questions and doubts. He anguished over how he could ever be saved. His inner torment kept him awake at night, but he continued his search for meaning. He searched through the bible, he prayed, he sought counsel from others.

Finally one day he found the key to his search for

peace. He was reading St. Paul's Letter to the Romans and stopped short at verse 21 of chapter 1: "The just man shall live by faith."

At last he found an answer to his anxiety. It is through faith in God's grace that it is possible to be saved. Salvation is God's gift, not the result of personal achievement. Therefore, one needs to trust oneself to God's love.

What followed in Luther's life grew out of this radical insight into the importance of faith in God, whose love and grace reach man through Jesus Christ. The two facets—faith and grace—are complementary. One can only place one's life trustingly in God's hands if one is deeply convinced of his love, his grace. His grace in turn enables man to believe. As St. Paul wrote to the Christians at Rome: "All depends on faith, everything is grace" (Rom 4:16).

Insight into the role of faith brought some measure of peace to Luther's anguished spirit. He shared his insight with his students and with his fellow theologians. Gradually, for a variety of reasons, his teaching and preaching led to confrontation with Church authorities. Christianity was divided in spite of Luther's intent. Heated argument on both sides solidified mutual misunderstandings and false interpretations.

Today, after the polemic fog is lifted, and serious efforts at ecumenism progress, it becomes clearer how sound and traditional Luther's germinal idea was. It is through faith that man can hope for salvation. Faith that trustingly opens the mind and heart of God's saving grace or love. In fact, Luther's emphasis on faith and grace is close to the heart of the New Testament (and Old Testament) message.

St. Paul, who anguished through the same kind of inner struggle Luther experienced, pointed out that it is not the law, nor ritual, that is most important. The one thing that counts for anything, he wrote to the Galatians, is "only faith, which expresses itself in love" (Gal 5:6). Or as he writes so clearly to the Ephesians: "I repeat, it is owing to his favor that salvation is yours through faith" (Eph 2:8).

Recalling other New Testament passages we discover that a person becomes mature in faith by becoming like a child—trusting and open. Faith recognizes that there is more to life than any man can grasp or control. Faith admits that God is greater than man's heart.

The person of faith places himself, his life, his future in God's hands, fully confident that his grace is sufficient. By faith we recognize that God is not angry with us. Faith allows us to hope.

While differences still remain between Roman Catholics and Lutherans, we are mutually discovering that many of the differences rest on mutual misunderstandings. We can be grateful to Luther and the great Lutheran tradition for preserving so clearly a central part of Christ's gospel, namely, that the just man lives by faith. Faith expresses itself, for Catholic and Lutheran alike, in justice, love, and service.

Today Luther's wish is approaching realization: "I beg that my name be passed over in silence, and that men will call themselves not Lutherans but Christians. What is Luther? My teaching is not mine. . . . Let us root out party names and call ourselves Christians, for it is Christ's gospel we have."

QUESTIONS

1. T. or F.—Sixty-five million Lutherans are concentrated in Germany, the Scandinavian countries of Sweden, Norway, Denmark and Finland, Brazil, Argentina and the United States.

2. Martin Luther was a member of the . . . . order.

3. Lutheranism rests on two fundamental principles: Man is restored to friendship with God by . . . . in Jesus Christ alone, and the . . . . is the only source and guide of faith and life.

4. T. or F.—Martin Luther's intention was to divide Christianity.

5. It was . . . . who wrote: ". . . it is owing to His favor that salvation is yours through faith" (Eph 2:8).

6. T. or F.—We can be grateful to Luther and the great Lutheran tradition for preserving so clearly a central part of Christ's Gospel, namely that the just man lives by faith.

chapter 7 / the presbyterians

1

PRESBYTERIANISM takes its name from its form of church government and its theology from a 16th-century French lawyer and reformer, John Calvin. The various Protestant Churches in this tradition are known as Presbyterian, Reformed or Calvinist. Besides the 4,500,000 Presbyterians in the United States there are substantial numbers in Scotland, Holland, South Africa, Switzerland, France, and northern Ireland and smaller numbers in Germany, Hungary, England, and mission fields.

The name "Presbyterian" comes from a Greek word meaning "elder." Within the congregation the minister is known as the teaching elder while a group of elected and ordained laity are called the ruling elders. Together they form the session and 20 to 30 sessions comprise a presbytery which corresponds to a diocese. The Presbyterian system rejects the authority of bishops but unlike the Baptists and strict Congregationalists it recognizes a ruling body beyond the local church.

John Calvin left the study of law to embark on a career of church reform in 1533. At the age of 27 he published his *Institutes of the Christian Religion,* a classic of Reformed theology. In it Calvin emphasized the sovereignty of God and carried the idea of predestination to a conclusion which neither Catholics nor Lutherans reached. He reasoned that God both elects some souls to heaven and damns others to hell. Christ died only for those predestined to salvation.

From France Calvin moved to Geneva, Switzerland, where he set up a strict theocracy. His interpretation of the Christian life stressed industry, thrift, godliness, and sober living. After a few years the citizens rebelled against his thoroughgoing rule and sent Calvin into exile, but he was eventually invited back and ruled the city from 1541 until his death in 1564.

A onetime Catholic priest, John Knox embraced Calvinist principles during a stay in Geneva. Returning to his native Scotland he challenged the Catholic Queen Mary Stuart and succeeded in establishing Presbyterianism as the state religion.

In England the Presbyterian wing of the Puritan party gained control of Parliament and convoked the Westminster Assembly in 1643. During a five-year period these divines prepared the Westminster Confession which became the doctrinal statement of Scottish, English, and American Presbyterianism. The Confession reaffirmed Calvin's views on predestination: "By the decree of God, for the manifestation of his glory, some men and angels are predestined unto everlasting life, and others foreordained to everlasting death."

Scotch-Irish, English, and Dutch immigrants brought Presbyterianism to America and Christians of these nationalities remain the mainstays of the major Reformed bodies in the U.S. Eleven signers of the Declaration of Independence were Presbyterians and English loyalists often referred to the American Revolution as the Presbyterian Rebellion.

Presbyterians insisted on a college-educated ministry and were outstripped by the enthusiasm of Baptists and Methodists in carrying their denomination to the West and South and to the black community. Schisms and bitter theological battles also handicapped the growth of Presbyterianism. The Southern synods withdrew in 1857 over the issue of slavery; Northern and Southern branches have not been able thus far to heal this division.

Largest Presbyterian Church in this country is the 3,373,890-member United Presbyterian Church in the U.S.A. Contemporary Presbyterians honor the genius of Calvin and the historical importance of the Westminster Confession but seldom follow his theology in such questions as total depravity and double predestination.

The Presbyterian Church in the U.S. is the Southern branch of the Presbyterian tradition and reflects a more conservative theological and social stance. It reports 958,195 adherents. Seven smaller Presbyterian bodies enroll about 175,000 members. Two denominations of Dutch heritage also base their theology and policy on Calvinism: the Reformed Church in America (383,000) and the strict Christian Reformed Church (281,000).

The teaching elder or pastor preaches the word of God and administers the two sacraments of Baptism and the Lord's Supper. The ruling elders are elected and ordained, as are the deacons who are charged with helping the poor and needy.

At least three presbyteries make up a synod. The synods form the General Assembly which has customarily met each year. The democratic and representative structure of Presbyterians exerted a significant influence on the development of American political life.

2

My very learned lawyer friend went into a pout rather than attempt to answer my simple question. Several couples were meeting regularly with me to study the bible twice a month. This particular evening we were exploring the story of Abraham in the book of Genesis. After the group had shared their impressions of the story, I asked: "I wonder why God chose Abraham." That's when my normally loquacious attorney put on a glum face, shifted about nervously, and refused to say a word.

His reaction was understandable and honest. Rather than attempt glib answers, he preferred silence for my simple question touched one of the deepest mysteries of life. The question about Abraham bears down on each person, because the story of Abraham is also about every man. "Why did God choose me?" People have grappled with that question of choice or election for centuries. "Am I saved by God or by my own actions?"

John Calvin had a very clear, precise answer. "We assert that by an eternal and immutable counsel, God has once and for all determined, both whom he would admit to salvation, and whom he would condemn to destruction." This complete option for God's predominant role in man's destiny became the theological foundation of the Presbyterian tradition within Protestantism. This was some four centuries ago.

The intervening 400 years have mellowed that seemingly harsh view. Twentieth-century Presbyterianism has modified Calvin's position on predestination even to the point of rejecting it in its original form.

The proposed new Presbyterian confession of faith affirms that salvation occurs when divine love heals the conflicts that separate man from God. Man is responsible for his response to that healing love. No one ends up in hell or heaven except as a result of his free moral choices.

Although the interpretation of Calvin's teaching has so radically changed, the focus of his teaching remains characteristic of the Presbyterian tradition. Calvin focused on God's sovereign role in man's salvation.

Presbyterians today echo that emphasis on the primacy of God and his love in man's efforts to grow in Christian life. Personal responsibility for one's actions is preserved, but man does not save himself by his own efforts. Salvation, wholeness, holiness depends on God's healing, saving love.

In an age of excessive humanism this awareness of God's initiative in man's life is refreshing and sound. It recalls the beautiful insight of the psalmist, "Unless the Lord build the house, they labor in vain who build it" (Ps 127:1). Or the teaching of St. Paul to the Christians at Ephesus: "It is owing to his favor, that salvation is yours through faith. This is not your own doing, it is God's gift; neither is it a reward for anything you have accomplished, so let no one pride himself on it" (Eph 2:8-9).

Our human efforts are necessary but not sufficient to make us whole. Wholeness, or holiness, is something for which we bear responsibility, but only as co-operators with God's enabling love. As Jesus reminds us in the Gospel according to John: "Apart from me you can do nothing" (Jn 15:5). Already ten centuries before Calvin the Church officially taught: "For such is God's goodness to men that he wills that his gifts be our merits, and that he will grant us an eternal reward for what he has given us."

You may be wondering how this answers the question I posed to my bible study group: "Why do you suppose God chose Abraham?" "Why did God choose me?" It does not answer the question, for no "answer" is possible in the face of so deep a mystery of human existence.

Faced with that mystery, Presbyterianism—in many ways closer today to Roman Catholic tradition than to John Calvin—reminds us where to focus our attention, namely on God more than on man. Presbyterians and Roman Catholics believe that God's love takes the initiative in man's wholeness and holiness, in man's salvation. Both believe that man is responsible for how he responds to that love, and that reward or punishment hangs on his own free choices.

Both believe further that man's good choices, while truly his own, are made possible by God's love. Ultimately both pause in silent wonder before the mystery of God's love for us, conscious of the responsibility that love brings: "God chose us in him before the world began, to be holy and blameless in his sight, to be full of love" (Eph 1:4).

QUESTIONS

1. T. or F.—The Presbyterian religion was founded by John Calvin.

2. The name "presbyterian" comes from a Greek word meaning . . . .

3. The Presbyterian religion acknowledges the two sacraments of . . . . and the Eucharist.

4. T. or F.—The story of Abraham applies to everyone.

5. The proposed new Presbyterian confession of faith affirms that . . . . occurs when divine love heals the conflicts that separate man from God.

6. The phrase, "Unless the Lord build the house, they labor in vain who build it," is found in the Book of . . . .
   a) Psalms   b) Genesis   c) Ruth

chapter 8 / the / episcopalians

1

WHILE LUTHER AND CALVIN challenged the authority of the Catholic Church on theological grounds those who engineered the break with Rome in England were primarily motivated by political reasons. The king wanted to sever the ties between the English Church and the pope.

What evolved after the schism begun by Henry VIII has been known as the Church of England or the Anglican Church. In the United States it has been called the Protestant Episcopal or sometimes simply the Episcopal Church. Some 18 national churches in union with the Archbishop of Canterbury form the worldwide 40-million-member Anglican Communion.

In Anglicanism the form of church government—bishops, priests, and deacons—was carried over from Roman Catholicism. Much of the liturgy, creeds, piety and customs of Catholicism was also preserved. Many Episcopalians view their Church as both Catholic and Protestant.

Christianity had been introduced to the British Isles as early as the second century. Pope Gregory the Great sent St. Augustine to the island in 597 and he became the first Archbishop of Canterbury. During the 1,000 years from Augustine to Henry VIII the spiritual authority of the bishop of Rome had been acknowledged by kings and bishops alike.

When news of the Lutheran revolt reached England Henry VIII was moved to pen a theological attack on the new theology which earned him the papal title "Defender of the Faith." English sovereigns still receive this title at their coronation.

But when Henry found himself frustrated in attempts to win an annulment from the pope of his 18-year marriage to Catherine of Aragon he decided to claim headship of the Church in his realm. In 1543 he demanded that the English bishops and clergy reject papal authority. Only one bishop, John Fisher, resisted his demand; along with Sir Thomas More he paid for this disobedience with his life. The pope excommunicated the king.

In matters of doctrine and piety Henry VIII remained a traditional Catholic who opposed Protestant innovations such as the marriage of priests. Yet he suppressed hundreds of monasteries and persecuted any Englishmen who persisted in loyalty to the pope. Under the boy-king Edward VI and Queen Elizabeth the Church of England would be carried further into the Protestant camp.

Anglicans based their liturgy on the Book of Common Prayer and subscribed to the doctrinal statements in the Thirty-nine Articles adopted in 1571.

The Oxford movement of the mid-19th century not only led many Anglicans such as John Henry Newman to Rome but brought back a significant number of Anglicans to more Catholic thought and practices. The latter formed the High Church and Anglo-Catholic schools within Anglicanism.

Carried to America as early as 1607 Anglicanism became the established church in five of the original colonies. Lacking any bishops or diocesan organization for its first 177 years on this soil the Anglican Church was severely handicapped. Any communicant who desired confirmation or ordination had to return to England.

Most Anglican ministers were Tories who supported the head of their church, George III, during the American revolution; they fled to Canada and England after the war. Yet many patriots were also Anglicans: George Washington, Alexander Hamilton, Patrick Henry, and others. Stripped of its tax support and most of its clergy the Protestant Episcopal Church, now autonomous, counted only 30,000 members by 1830. Episcopalians made only feeble efforts to evangelize the frontier.

Today the Episcopal Church numbers about 3,285,000 members in this country and has traditionally found its greatest strength among the wealthy and those on the Eastern seaboard.

In an Episcopal parish the chief form of worship is known as the Holy Communion, the Eucharist, or the Mass. All Episcopalians recognize the two sacraments of Baptism and the Lord's Supper and many also attach a sacramental importance to the other five Catholic sacraments.

Hundreds of thousands of Episcopalians favor the Anglo-Catholic tradition which shares many positions with Roman Catholicism. These Episcopalians cultivate Catholic devotions, support Episcopalian religious orders for men and women including Benedictines and Franciscans, and view with suspicion attempts to merge their Church with Protestant denominations.

Official Anglican-Roman Catholic commissions have been meeting to examine doctrines and chart a path to reunion. In 1972 such a consultation announced "substantial agreement on the doctrine of the Eucharist." *The Decree on Ecumenism* singled out Anglicanism when it stated, "Among those (Churches) in which Catholic traditions and institutions in part continue to exist, the Anglican Communion occupies a special place."

2

I still remember Christmas Day many years ago. I was sick in bed, and spent most of the day watching television. Late in the morning there was what I would have taken to be a Roman Catholic Mass, except that it was in English. The hymns were familiar, the altar with its candles and flowers looked familiar, the priest wore vestments like those at my neighborhood parish.

There were readings from the bible, a sermon, the creed professing belief in the "one, holy, catholic and apostolic Church," the bread and wine, the words of consecration, communion, blessing—all so familiar to me. Yet I wasn't sure how the Mass could be in English (this was years ago!). Only at the end did the announcer mention that the liturgy was celebrated in the Episcopalian cathedral in New York!

Since that surprising discovery of how much Roman Catholics and Episcopalians shared in common, I have become more aware of the existing closeness between the two Churches. Unlike most Protestant Churches, the Episcopal Church retains much of Roman Catholic ritual and structure, and finds little quarrel with most of the doctrinal teachings of Roman Catholic tradition.

Since that Christmas I have made another discovery about Episcopalianism. Within the one Episcopal Church there are surprising differences in doctrine and ritual. In fact, Episcopalians exhibit a broader spectrum of pluralism than most major Protestant Churches. There is the "high church" or "Anglo-Catholic," which is so strikingly similar to the Roman Catholic in teaching and worship. Such was the Christmas Mass I watched on television.

But there is also the "low church" or evangelical group. Their worship appears little different from that of a Methodist congregation. Instead of Mass or Holy Communion the more typical service is Morning Prayer. Still a third branch within the Episcopal Church is the "broad" or "modernist." A typical sermon in a congregation of this branch might fit equally well in a Unitarian service.

This surprising pluralism within the one Protestant Episcopal Church (or Anglican Church in England) strikes me as worth reflecting on. How can one Church tolerate such wide differences of teaching and ritual? How can unity be preserved with such plurality? The Episcopalian experience suggests to me the important distinction between unity and uniformity.

Episcopalians clearly value unity. They preserve the hierarchical structure of the Church, and are increasingly open to the role of the pope as a principle of unity. Episcopalian theologians recognize only one Catholic Church. However, they view that one Church as made up of four branches: Roman Catholic, Anglican, Eastern Orthodox, and Old Catholic. In their own branch, the Anglican or Episcopal, they recognize the "high," "low," and "broad" communities. Unity is not identified with uniformity.

This aspect of Episcopal tradition deserves serious thought. We Roman Catholics have tended consciously or unconsciously to identifying unity and uniformity. Uniformity was reflected in the catechisms from Baltimore to Bangkok, in the celebration of the Mass in Boston or Borneo, in the average sermon in most parishes the world over.

Today this is no longer true, and one may fear that

the loss of uniformity in ritual and religion texts necessarily means the loss of Catholic unity. The example of the Episcopal Church's enduring unity with recognized plurality, should caution against an overly hasty identification of unity with uniformity. To be one does not require being the same.

QUESTIONS

1. T. or F.—In England, the Episcopalian religion is called the Anglican religion.

2. The founder of the Anglican religion in England was King . . . . the Eighth.

3. T. or F.—In Anglicanism the form of church government was carried over from Roman Catholicism.

4. Within the one Episcopal Church there are surprising . . . . in doctrine and ritual.

5. T. or F.—The Episcopalian and Roman Catholic Churches have much in common.

6. The Episcopalian Church, within its own branch, recognizes the "high" and "low" and " . . . . " communities.

chapter 9/the baptists

1

HOW AND WHEN a person is baptized has been a central concern for several centuries for the Christians known as Baptists. They believe that only adults should receive Baptism and that the only proper form is immersion. They reject such practices as the baptism of infants or the pouring or sprinkling of water in administering the ordinance.

Besides the Baptists many other Churches prefer immersion, including the Disciples of Christ, Churches of Christ, Brethren, Mennonites, Seventh-day Adventists, and Mormons. Sometimes the baptism will be held in a river or pond and at other times in a baptismal pool in the church building. Until the 13th century immersion was the normal form of Baptism in Roman Catholicism and it remains an acceptable form in the Western Church as well as in Eastern Orthodoxy.

Beyond their special views on Baptism the Baptists reject any spiritual authority above that of the individual congregation. The congregation has the authority to call and discharge the preacher, determine the form of worship, elect elders and deacons, and admit new members. Baptists proclaim "No human founder, no human authority, no human creed." Only the bible can bind the conscience of the Baptist believer.

Baptist beliefs can be traced to the persecuted Anabaptists of the 16th century. Forming what has been called the left wing of the Reformation, these Anabaptists preached that only adult believers could declare their personal faith in Christ and, therefore, receive the baptism which symbolized this decision. A small group of English dissenters formed a Baptist Church in Amsterdam in 1609.

Roger Williams founded the first Baptist Church in America in Providence, Rhode Island, in 1639. Williams remained a Baptist for only a few months; he spent the rest of his life as a Seeker. But the seed was planted and the Baptist movement registered great gains in later years, especially during the 19th century.

Disputes over slavery divided the Baptists in 1845 and gave rise to the Southern Baptist Convention which has since become the largest single Protestant Church in the nation. Southern Baptist congregations have been organized in all 50 states and baptize about 1,000 new members every day of the year.

Southern Baptists have been distinguished by their energetic evangelistic programs, extensive Sunday-school system, and conservative theology. Billy Graham, a Southern Baptist minister, is probably the best-known Protestant clergyman in the country and one of the most successful revivalists. Not enthusiastic about the ecumenical search for more visible church unity, the Southern Baptists have stayed out of the National and World Councils of Churches.

With fewer than 1,500,000 members the American Baptist Church, formerly known as the Northern Baptists, tolerates a wider range of theological opinion. These Baptists have made substantial contributions to local, national, and world church councils.

Baptist worship tends to be simple and informal and features the sermon, gospel hymns, and scripture reading. The average Baptist congregation will observe the Lord's Supper four times a year as a memorial service.

2

Somehow it was leaked to the news media that Harry Truman, while President of the United States, from time to time enjoyed a good shot of whiskey. Most people at the time took the revelation in stride, but not all. Some influential Baptists launched an effort to have the President, himself a Baptist, expelled from the Southern Baptist Convention because of his occasional nip.

Truman responded in typically blunt fashion. He pointed out in no uncertain language that no one in the Convention had any power to expel him or anyone else. Although no theologian, Truman was right.

This was not a matter of executive privilege, but of sound Baptist principles. Baptist Churches have no right or procedures for excommunicating members or enforcing ethical or doctrinal standards. As a Baptist, Harry Truman stood up for his freedom of conscience which is a central part of Baptist tradition.

Perhaps nothing is more characteristic of Baptists in America than their jealous concern about freedom of conscience and religious liberty. For Baptists it is a deeply held conviction that no one has spiritual authority over the individual believer.

Only God and the bible bind the Baptist's conscience. There are no creeds, no sacraments, no ecclesiastical systems of government, no prescribed ritual. Baptists are religiously democratic because faith is necessarily a free commitment. For that same reason they refuse to baptize infants.

The Baptist insistence on religious liberty and individual freedom is something to be admired, something for which we Americans can be grateful. The fact that the Baptist interpretation of this radically Christian principle differs from that of other Christian Churches including our own, need not diminish either our admiration or our gratitude. In fact, the Baptist respect for personal freedom and recognition of personal responsibility can stimulate us to look more deeply at our own awareness of individual religious rights and responsibilities.

As the Second Vatican Council reminded us, freedom of conscience is the other side of personal responsibility, and faith is of necessity free. "For its part, authentic freedom is an exceptional sign of the divine image within man. For God has willed that man be left 'in the hand of his own counsel' so that he can seek his Creator spontaneously, and come freely to utter and blissful perfection through loyalty to him.

"Hence man's dignity demands that he act according to a knowing and free choice. Such a choice is personally motivated and prompted from within. It does not result from blind internal impulse, nor from mere external pressure" *(Church Today,* 17).

It would be well worth the time to read the Council's fuller treatment of religious liberty, namely the *Declaration on Religious Freedom.* It is a uniquely American contribution to the Council, created chiefly by the late John Courtney Murray, S.J., out of his years of theological reflection on religious freedom within the American democratic experience. The Council states: "God calls men to serve him in spirit and in truth. Hence they are bound in conscience but they stand under no compulsion . . . man is to be guided by his own judgment and he is to enjoy freedom" (11).

Undoubtedly Roman Catholic and Baptist interpretations of the shared Christian principle of individual freedom differ. However, before emphasizing the differences, it can be helpful to reflect more deeply on one's own religious tradition of religious liberty.

QUESTIONS

1. T. or F.—Members of the Baptist religion believe that only adults should receive Baptism.

2. For Baptists, ... is the proper form of Baptism.

3. Only the . . . . can bind the conscience of the Baptist believer.

4. T. or F.—Baptists have no right or procedures for excommunicating members or enforcing ethical standards.

5. Baptists in America are characterized by a great concern for freedom of conscience and . . . . liberty.

6. Baptists have no . . . . : a) creeds, b) sacraments, c) prescribed rituals, d) all of these.

chapter 10/the united
/church of christ

1

MEMBERS OF THE United Church of Christ can claim as their spiritual ancestors both the Pilgrim Fathers who landed on Plymouth Rock in 1620 and groups of German Calvinists who came to these shores in the 18th and 19th centuries. The present Church was formed in 1957 through a union of the Congregational Christian Churches and the Evangelical and Reformed Church.

Both partners in the 1957 merger were themselves the result of earlier church unions. The blending of German and English traditions, of Presbyterian and Congregational forms of church government give the two-million-member United Church of Christ a distinctive character.

To understand the UCC we must examine the religious beliefs and practices of the Christians who formed the Churches involved in the merger.

In 17th-century England various dissidents felt that the established Church of England had not gone far enough to embrace the theology of the Reformation and to purify itself of "popish" elements. Most of these preferred to remain within the Anglican Church and were known as Puritans. Some more radical critics came to believe that Anglicanism would never adopt their views; they decided to separate themselves from this Church and to organize their own religious communities.

One such group of Separatists had fled persecution in England and settled in Holland. Unwilling to become absorbed by the Dutch they set sail on the Mayflower for the New World.

While the Pilgrims built their homes at Plymouth, groups of Puritans who numbered 20,000 by 1640 established the nearby Massachusetts Bay Colony. Eventually the Puritans abandoned all ties with Anglicanism and adopted the Congregational polity of the smaller Pilgrim settlement. They rejected the authority of any bishops or religious body beyond the local congregation. In matters of theology both Pilgrims and Puritans followed the stern teachings of John Calvin.

Dominating the religious scene in New England the Congregationalists founded some of the most prestigious colleges in America: Harvard, Yale, Dartmouth, and others. In their theocracy only Church members could vote in civil elections but all citizens had to pay taxes to support the Congregational Church. Persecuted in England, they in turn persecuted Quakers, Baptists, and other dissenters when they gained control of the colonies of New England.

Congregationalism lost its opportunity to remain the chief religious force in the new nation. Influential clergy and Churches left the mother Church to form the Unitarian movement in 1825; almost all of the Congregational Churches in Boston accepted Unitarianism. A cooperative arrangement with the Presbyterians allowed the latter to spread throughout the West at the expense of Congregationalism. Congregationalists sought to convert the American Indians and even managed to re-create a New England theocracy in Hawaii but the energetic Methodists, Baptists and Disciples of Christ won far more adherents in the Midwest and South.

In 1931 the Congregationalists joined forces with a small denomination called the Christian Church, sometimes called the Baptist Unitarians. The new entity took the name, Congregational Christian Churches.

German immigrants leaning toward a Calvinist rather than a Lutheran theology founded the Reformed Church in the United States. Other German Calvinists organized the Evangelical Synod in 1840. These two bodies united in 1934 to form the Evangelical and Reformed Church.

When the Congregational Church and the Evangelical and Reformed Church began to investigate merger possibilities a compromise in Church government was required. In contrast to the Congregational system the Evangelical and Reformed Church followed a form of Presbyterian government. In the words of Douglas Horton, "The New England boiled dinner and the Pennsylvania sauerkraut had to come to terms with each other."

Negotiations continued for many years and law suits delayed the final merger. Even after the merger a number of Congregational Churches refused to surrender their former independence; they have set up new Congregational associations outside the United Church of Christ.

The strict Calvinism of the Puritans has given way to one of the most liberal statements in American Protestantism. No one need subscribe to any set of doctrines to gain or hold membership in the UCC. Likewise a wide latitude is given local congregations in matters of worship. Puritan abhorrence of vestments, candles, stained glass and the like has not prevented a program of liturgical enrichment in the 1970's.

Because of the different ethnic backgrounds of the partners in the 1957 union and the successful compromise of two forms of Church government the creation of the United Church of Christ has been a unique achievement in American Protestantism.

2

For six years I have appeared regularly on an ecumenical television program. Each week Dr. Edward Bauman and a group of panelists spend an hour before TV cameras exploring some part of the bible within the context of contemporary life.

Dr. Bauman is a Methodist minister; the rest of us come from various Christian traditions. Each year the ecumenical mix has varied, including Roman Catholic, Southern Baptists, Disciples of Christ, Lutheran, Episcopalian, Methodist and Church of the Savior.

It has been a rewarding experience. The first year my reaction was one of genuine surprise at how much we shared in common. Gradually, differences became more obvious, but never overshadowed the experienced unity. Somehow the existing differences of theological interpretation, traditional language, and church structures paled in the face of a shared commitment to Christ and a mutual respect.

Yet the divisions remain and cannot simply be ignored. In a very real sense we are one in sharing a deep faith in Jesus Christ. In just as real a sense we are not united in our worship. Together on the TV set each Friday afternoon, we are separated into different churches on Sunday morning. The question comes: How can unity become more real, while remaining faithful to our personal convictions and differing traditions?

I do not profess to know any simple answers to that question. Dialogue between official representatives of the Roman Catholic Church and of various Protestant Churches is going forward slowly but seriously. On the level of persons sharing common tasks, as those of us on the TV show each week, bonds of unity arise that respect yet bridge differences. Christians the world over increasingly pray with Jesus Christ: "that their unity may be complete" (Jn 17:23). Few Roman Catholic ecumenists today expect Christian unity to occur simply by everyone converting to the Church of Rome.

It is in the light of that movement toward unity, with centuries of misunderstandings to be bridged and deeply felt doctrinal and devotional traditions to be respected, that the existence of the United Church of Christ seems significant. Not that it presents the model for ecumenical unity, but it does suggest some of the ideals and complexities of growing unity among Christians.

In 1957 the United Church of Christ was formed in a fashion unique in American Protestantism. Two Churches with different traditions merged into one new Church. The Congregationalist Church, brought to this country from England by the Pilgrims, united with the Evangelical and Reformed Church, tracing its past to German immigrants.

The differences between the two Churches went deeper than national origins. Congregationalists recognized no authority beyond the local congregation. The Evangelical and Reformed had a modified Presbyterian form of Church organization to which individual congregations were subject. In doctrine, too, they differed although both found their roots in Calvinist theology. No creed of any kind could bind individual Congregationalist members, while the Evangelical and Reformed followed Luther's Catechism and the Augsburg Confession.

Differences were so deeply felt in spite of the bond of faith in Christ which they shared, that the merger took 15 years of careful work. For five years a minority of Congregationalists blocked the union by taking court action. They lost their case and the merger took place, although some 100,000 Congregationalists refused to join the new United Church of Christ.

The fact that two Christian Churches with many points of difference in structure, ritual and teaching could find a way to organic unity appears to me to be a sign of hope, as well as a reminder of the difficulties to be encountered, on the way to Christian unity. The United Church of Christ is a living symbol of the fact that differences can be resolved into a deeper unity.

QUESTIONS

1. T. or F.—The United Church of Christ was formed by a merger of the Catholic and Congregational religions.

2. In New England, the Congregationalists founded . . . . : a) Harvard, b) Yale, c) Dartmouth, d) all of these.

3. In matters of theology both Pilgrims and Puritans followed the stern teaching of John . . . .

4. T. or F.—Despite all the advances made in ecumenism, there still remain many differences between the various religions.

5. The Congregational religion was brought to this country by the . . . .

6. T. or F.—Before they merged, the only difference between the Congregational and Evangelical Churches was national origin.

chapter 11/the quakers

1

DEDICATION TO THE principle of pacifism characterizes several Christian denominations including the
Mennonite Church, the Church of the Brethren and
the Society of Friends (the Quakers). They insist that a
true follower of Christ will never take up arms but will
lead a life of nonviolence.

Worldwide the Quakers number no more than
200,000 but their witness for peace, social justice and
humanitarianism gives them an influence far beyond
their size. The 122,000 American Quakers belong to a
dozen groups or Meetings with varying theological
orientations.

The Quaker believes he must direct his life according to the Inner Light. This is not conscience but that
which enlightens conscience. Quaker theologians
sometimes describe this Inner Light as "that of God in
each man." The Quaker seeks such direct divine illumination by quiet prayer and meditation. The Society
of Friends has jettisoned the means to salvation offered by other Christian traditions: baptism and the
other sacraments, ritual, priesthood, formal prayers.

In traditional Quakerism the central act of worship
is the silent meeting. Members come together at the
appointed time on First Day (Sunday) and sit quietly in

silence for an hour or so. A few times during the period the silence may be broken by someone's personal testimony or spiritual thought. The familiar components in Protestant and Catholic worship are missing: sermon, hymns, scripture readings, set prayers, communion.

Once a month the congregation gathers for a business meeting. Appointed elders and overseers carry out the duties normally performed by a clergyman. Women hold equal power with men in Quaker assemblies.

In some Quaker congregations in the Middle West, West and South the silent meeting has been replaced by a programmed worship service not much different from any Protestant denomination. These groups, usually identified as Friends Churches, are often served by salaried Quaker ministers rather than by unpaid volunteers.

George Fox (1624-1691) founded the Society of Friends. As a young man he left the established Anglican Church and wandered around England seeking greater religious enlightenment. Gradually he developed his concept of the Inner Light and other distinctive Quaker beliefs and practices. His followers would not wage war, swear oaths, acknowledge social distinctions, or pay tithes to the state Church. Fox ascribed to the Inner Light the normative role accorded the bible by other Protestants.

Fox and the early Quakers faced harsh persecution as they sought to win converts in England, Ireland, and elsewhere. Fox himself visited America in 1671-1673. Except in Rhode Island the Quakers found no welcome in the colonies; four Quakers were hanged in Boston for their religious convictions and others were whipped, tortured and deported.

William Penn, a convert to Quakerism, founded

Pennsylvania in 1681 and invited his coreligionists to settle there. They implemented their ideas of religious freedom in the colony, befriended the Indians, worked to abolish slavery.

After the American Revolution Quakerism lost most of its missionary zeal. Frequent purges reduced the ranks and few converts joined the sober Quakers. A religious schism in 1827 divided the Society of Friends into the Hicksites who favored a Unitarian position and the more orthodox Quakers. Conservatives sparked another division in 1845. Today the Quakers in the United States belong to three major and numerous smaller groupings. No Quaker group demands acceptance of any particular creed.

A Quaker generally avoids gambling and liquor. He can claim conscientious objector status if called to serve in the armed forces. Yet an estimated 8,000 American Quakers served in the Army and Navy during World War II; the tolerant Quakers did not expel these Quakers whose consciences led them to abandon nonviolence.

The tiny Quaker community has contributed two U.S. presidents during the past half century: Herbert Hoover and Richard M. Nixon. Nixon holds membership in a Friends Church in Whittier, California, and attended Whittier College, a Quaker institution.

In 1947 the American Friends Service Committee shared the Nobel peace prize with its British counterpart, the Friends Service Council. The AFSC coordinates Quaker efforts around the world to foster nonviolence and alleviate poverty, sickness, and ignorance.

2

Some years ago I was enjoying several days' vacation at Cape May, New Jersey, an old resort town on the Atlantic seacoast. It just happened that a national gathering of the Society of Friends, or Quakers, was taking place at Cape May at the same time.

Mingling with the many Quakers on the boardwalk, I found them open and friendly, as their official name, Friends, suggested they might be. I even felt very welcome at one of their prayer meetings, although I was somewhat uncomfortable and unsure of what might happen.

A group of 15 or 20 men and women arranged themselves in wicker chairs on the hotel porch overlooking the seemingly endless ocean. I sat on the side observing. No one spoke. Gradually the stillness deepened. Everyone was silent. Then, to my surprise, a middle-aged woman began to describe her experience of God. No one seemed to notice her, although it was evident that all listened carefully to her. Then, silence again. Some minutes later an elderly man shared his thoughts and feelings about God's place in man's life. His words, too, seemed absorbed into the deep stillness. A young woman offered a brief, spontaneous prayer of thanks to God. Extended silence followed, broken once or twice by an expression of petition or thanks. At the end of about an hour, the meeting ended as simply as it had begun. All shook hands and the group split up.

Being present at their prayer meeting was a moving experience. I later learned that silence was their only ritual — no sermons, hymn singing or group vocal prayer. Their effort was to open themselves through silence to experience the Inner Light of God. Friends

or Quakers believe that the Inner Light is the immediate influence of the Holy Spirit on individuals.

Their founder, George Fox, believed that God gave
the Inner Light to each person and that it was experienced in stillness.

A famous Quaker wrote that "Friends are not much
interested in abstract theories and statements about
God. They prefer to begin with personal experience of
him." The personal experience of the Light of God's
Holy Spirit is at the heart of Quaker faith. A Quaker
committee directly stated that "this direct contact between the Spirit of Christ and the human spirit, we are
prepared to trust to as the basis of our individual and
corporate life."

From my experience at their prayer meeting, and
from study afterwards, I came to admire the Quaker
focus on the Inner Light, perceived in silence. More
recently I became conscious of another dimension of
the Quaker spirit. For over a year I occasionally passed
a group of Quakers keeping vigil in front of the White
House. Whether I walked by in rain or shine, winter
or summer, morning or evening, they were there si-
lently protesting against the Vietnam war.

It was from that steadfast public witness against
war that I began to learn of the immense Quaker commitment to a wide variety of social concerns. Quakers
have been outstanding in their struggle against war and
every form of discrimination or injustice. Symbolic of
this commitment to social justice was the dramatic
action of Quakers in the Pennsylvania State Assembly
of 1756. Rather than vote for a war against the Indians
they voluntarily gave up their seats and political control of Pennsylvania.

Since the earliest days of their presence in the
American colonies Quakers have established a remarkable record of furthering causes like the abolition of

slavery, proper health care for the poor, aged and emotionally disturbed, equality of the sexes, disaster relief, care of conscientious objectors, racial justice, and peace among nations.

Although the basic Quaker attention to individually perceiving the Inner Light of God in silent prayer has at times led to a kind of self-centered quietism, the most authentic Quaker spirit finds in silent contact with the Inner Light the courage and guidance needed to come to grips with the serious social issues of the world in which they live. As Quaker statesman William Penn wrote, "True godliness does not turn men out of the world, but enables them to live better in it and excites their endeavors to mend it."

It is perhaps this creative balance between personal, silent prayer and dynamic social action that I find most meaningful in the witness of the Friends or Quakers. Their attitude toward silence and active social involvement, between personal contemplation and collaborative social action, has deep roots in the common tradition of Christians. Jesus himself reveals a healthy interplay of solitary prayer in the deserts and mountains of Palestine and tireless activity for the sick and poor in the towns and villages. His example has been a living model for Christians down through the centuries.

Today as many more Christians are rediscovering the Holy Spirit and informal prayer, the Quaker experience suggests a wordless warning against preoccupation with self in one's search for God's Light. Likewise as more and more Christians become increasingly involved in the pressing social and political issues of our time, the Friends are smiling witnesses that without personal contact with the spirit in stillness, the roots of sustained social action may well dry up or be turned to self-seeking. The Inner Light of the

Holy Spirit and the helping hand of active Christian compassion are but two sides of the authentic experience of him whom all Christians embrace as the "true Light of the World."

QUESTIONS

1. The Mennonite Church, the Church of the Brethren, and the Society of Friends (also called . . . .) hold a common belief in a life of . . . .

2. T. or F.—The Quakers look to "the Inner Light" for direction in addition to relying on help from the sacraments.

3. The Quaker community in America has produced two Presidents: 1) . . . . and 2) . . . .

4. T. or F.—Silence is the only ritual of a typical Quaker prayer meeting.

5. Quakers believe that the . . . . is the immediate influence of the . . . . on individuals.

6. T. or F.—The Quakers have achieved a balance between personal, silent prayer and dynamic, social action.

chapter 12/the
methodists

1

THE ESTABLISHED Church of England in the 18th century desperately needed reform and renewal. Morals, church attendance, and evangelism had sunk to low levels. The workingman rarely took any interest in the worship and life of the Anglican Church.

Into this situation came two remarkable brothers who sought to invigorate the Anglican Church of which they were priests. They crisscrossed England and Ireland organizing bible classes and taking the gospel to the common man. Eventually what started as a movement of spiritual renewal within Anglicanism became a separate Church: Methodism.

John Wesley was born in 1703, the 15th child of the Anglican rector at Epworth; his brother Charles was the 18th. As students at Oxford University the pair organized a Holy Club whose members agreed to form their personal lives through regular prayer, bible study, fasting, Holy Communion, and service to others. Their methodical regimen of devotions and ascetical practices won them the name Methodists.

After graduation from Oxford the Wesleys were ordained and set off for the colony of Georgia in 1732 to convert the Indians. Their missionary efforts were disappointing and they were dissatisfied with the fervor of their own spiritual lives. But while crossing the Atlantic they had been impressed by the calm faith of a band of Moravians, followers of the Bohemian reformer, John Hus.

Back in England in 1738 John Wesley happened to drop by a prayer meeting of Moravians on May 24. At this meeting he experienced a conversion of heart which was the real birth of Methodism.

Fired with enthusiasm John Wesley would spend the next 50 years traveling over 250,000 miles by foot and horseback preaching and organizing Methodist societies. The Anglican Churches were usually closed to Wesley and his fellow preachers but they preached instead in fields, factories, and mine pits. Wesley urged all Methodists to remain in the Church of England.

Charles Wesley also became famous as the author of some 6,000 hymns including, "Hark, the Herald Angels Sing."

Wesley's theology turned away from the strict predestination taught by the Calvinists. He believed that a Christian could actually aspire to perfection, complete freedom from sin. Wesley never claimed to have reached the state of perfection himself, but he insisted it was possible. His interpretation of the gospel was more hopeful, universal and optimistic than that of many other Protestants.

Methodist missionaries carried the movement to the American colonies, although most major Protestant denominations there had a 150-year head start. After the Revolution a majority of Anglican clergy returned to England and few remained to administer the sacraments to those who belonged to Methodist societies. Wesley agonized over the problem of ministering to American Methodists and finally decided that he himself would ordain ministers. He had been persuaded that the New Testament Church saw no distinction between priest and bishop.

The Methodist Episcopal Church was organized in Baltimore in 1784. Two leading ministers were given the title "bishop" although Wesley was displeased at the use of this title. The Methodists drew up 25 Articles of Religion, abridged from the Anglican 39 Articles. Their form of worship was modeled after the Book of Common Prayer.

Methodist circuit riders—bibles and hymn books in their saddlebags—carried the Wesleyan teachings to the frontier. Like the Baptists, the Methodists won many converts in the West and South.

Black Methodists formed the African Methodist Episcopal Church in 1816 as well as the A.M.E. Zion Church (1821) and the Colored (now Christian) Methodist Episcopal Church (1870). These three Churches now enroll about 2,500,000 black Methodists.

American Methodism also suffered divisions over the nature of bishops' authority and over the question of slavery, but the three major Methodist bodies reunited in 1939. Later a Church founded by German-speaking Methodists known as the Evangelical United Brethren merged with the Methodist Church to form the United Methodist Church. This Church reports about 11 million members.

Methodists have not placed much emphasis on matters of doctrine. Wesley himself said: "The distinguishing marks of a Methodist are not his opinions of any sort."

Methodism in this country has been characterized as middle class, activist, well organized, and theologically liberal. The Church still discourages smoking and drinking but is less inclined to make total abstinence the test of Christian fellowship.

2

Smiling John Wesley stretched out his hand to his opponent as he said: "If your heart is as my heart, then give me your hand." Taken aback momentarily by this surprising move after an hour-long heated argument, the other man finally shook hands. Their intense theological debate about whether people are predestined to heaven and hell or go there because of their own free choices ended, if not in agreement, at least in a sense of fellowship.

John Wesley, who is known as the founder of Methodism, was an Anglican priest and theologian at the time. His adversary in that argument some 250 years ago was a Calvinist theologian. Both were convinced that doctrine mattered, that theology was important.

But what characterized Wesley and the subsequent Methodist tradition is symbolized by his gesture. He felt that if his heart and that of the Calvinist were in the same place, there was no reason why they should be separated by doctrinal or theological differences. Doctrine was indeed important, but the experience of Christ, the experience of the Holy Spirit, provided a deeper and more vital bond than doctrinal agreement.

Methodist tradition has continued that placing of priority on experience over doctrine. There has been less stress on theology than on devotion, although theology has not been neglected. Methodists from Wesley's time to the present have paid particular attention to the action of the Holy Spirit in the experience of the individual as well as in the Church.

The beginning of the Methodist revival began with such an experience. It was May 24, 1738, during an evening religious meeting in London. John Wesley later recalled: "I felt my heart strangely warmed. I felt I did trust in Christ, Christ alone for salvation."

Deeply moved by the experience, he and his brother, Charles, also an Anglican priest, went out into the fields and into private homes to preach a revivalist, practical religion of hope, salvation and free will. Today American Methodists need not subscribe to any set creed, but need to promise loyalty to Christ.

The Methodist emphasis on experiencing Christ as more important than adhering to certain doctrinal definitions about Christ is admirable and radically sound. Roman Catholics may have serious problems with the complete doctrinal openness of contemporary Methodism, but may learn from the Methodist focus on experience. Actually, without relinquishing its genuine concern for doctrinal definition, the Second Vatican Council restored experience to its proper place in the Church.

In a very traditional sense doctrine is the expression or definition of the experience of God by the Christian community. St. John says he and the other apostles preach "what we have heard, what we have seen with our eyes . . . and our hands have touched," namely the Word of God, Jesus Christ (I Jn 1:1).

The experience of Christ necessarily precedes the definition of that experience. The object of faith, as no less a theologian than St. Thomas Aquinas pointed out, is not doctrinal formulations about God, but God himself, known and loved in a personal relationship.

Doctrine is important for many reasons, one of which is as an objective community check on one's subjective experience. But doctrine about Christ ultimately rests on experience of him and his Spirit. Methodism can help us be mindful of that as all Christians reach out their hands to fellow Christians in efforts at closer unity.

QUESTIONS

1. T. or F.—The founder of the Methodist Church was John Wesley.

2. Before becoming a separate church, the Methodist movement was part of the . . . . church.

3. Wesley was convinced that the New Testament Church saw no distinction between priest and . . . .

4. T. or F.—The Methodist tradition continues to place a priority on experience over doctrine.

5. In a very traditional sense . . . . is the expression or definition of the experience of God by the Christian community.

6. T. or F.—The object of faith is God himself, known and loved in a personal relationship.

chapter 13/the disciples
/of christ and
/churches of christ

1

AN EARLY 19TH-CENTURY movement which sought to restore primitive Christianity and unite all believers in a creedless fellowship resulted in the addition of two more denominations to the crowded religious scene in America. They are the Disciples of Christ and the Churches of Christ.

Concentrated in the Middle West and the South the Disciples report 1,425,000 members in about 8,000 congregations. In some communities their congregations are identified as simply the First Christian Church, Main Street Christian Church, etc. In some places they are known as the Church of Christ.

As early as 1792 James O'Kelly had led a small exodus from Methodism on the basis of a noncreedal platform. An ex-Presbyterian revivalist, Barton W. Stone, won converts to his near-Unitarian position in Kentucky and Ohio. Others around the country also came to believe that creeds and doctrines only divide Christians.

The Campbells, father and son, wielded the greatest influence in the frontier revival which gave birth to the Disciples of Christ. Thomas Campbell had been an Anglican and then a Presbyterian in his native northern Ireland. Emigrating to America he pastored a Presbyterian Church in Pennsylvania but his theological views led to a heresy trial. As a free-lance preacher he elaborated his basic positions such as, "No creed but Christ, no book but the bible" and "Where the scriptures speak, we speak; where the scriptures are silent, we are silent."

Joined by his son, Alexander, he formed a non-denominational association in 1809. Now the Campbells questioned not only the value of creeds but the validity of infant baptism. In 1812 the two were baptized by immersion and entered an affiliation with the Baptists which lasted for the next 17 years.

Much of the motivation for the efforts of Thomas and Alexander Campbell came from a search for Christian unity. Yet they insisted on baptism of adult believers by immersion as the only proper form of this ordinance. This meant that the baptism received by most professed Christians, Protestant and Catholic, was meaningless and invalid.

The Campbells joined forces with Barton Stone's followers in 1832 to form the Disciples of Christ. The fellowship grew and survived the Civil War without schism but by the time of the federal census of 1906 the conservative wing had broken from the parent body.

Those who organized the Churches of Christ shared many positions with the Disciples: baptism of believers by immersion, weekly communion, no creeds or confessions of faith, congregational autonomy. They differed on such matters as the use of pipe organs in worship and the formation of missionary societies, neither of which to them had any scriptural basis. They understood the silence of the scriptures to mean prohibition. Today the Churches of Christ display considerable enthusiasm for evangelism and missions but little for ecumenical cooperation.

Unlike the Churches of Christ, the Disciples take a leading role in the National and World Councils of Churches. Except for the custom of communion every Sunday the Disciples do not differ much from the American (Northern) Baptists. In some cities Disciples and Baptists have formed single congregations.

Some Disciples who remained in the parent body after the Churches of Christ people left were still troubled by the alleged liberalism of the Church. In 1927 these Disciples started to set up separate bible colleges, associations, and publications. They were sometimes called Restoratists or Independents.

Today about half of the Disciples support the North American Christian Convention. About 4,500 mainstream congregations contribute to the International Convention of Christian Churches (Disciples of Christ) with headquarters in Indianapolis.

Despite the apparent failure of the formula for Christian unity proposed by the Campbells and their associates, the Disciples of Christ remain committed to the New Testament ideal of unity. In the words of Stone, the long-range objective of the Disciples is to "die, be dissolved and sink into union with the body of Christ at large."

2

Several years ago I had the opportunity to visit Israel. Seventeen of us spent two weeks together traveling the length and breadth of the Holy Land. About half of our group were Roman Catholic, and the other half were members of other Christian Churches. Three were ministers whose familiarity with the bible was striking. Not only did they know countless gospel hymns— which they sang at the various places where the gospel story had unfolded centuries before—but the bible was a major influence on their day-to-day living.

I recall one afternoon talking with one of the ministers. It was at Caesarea Philippi where Jesus is said to have asked Peter: "Who do you say I am?" (Mt 16:13-20). Somewhat embarrassed at my ignorance, I asked the minister what denomination he belonged to. "I don't belong to any denomination. I belong to the Christian Church." Not satisfied, I questioned him further. He pointed out that the Church of Christ, or Christian Church, is not a denomination.

I pressed him as to what he believed, how he understood his identity as a member of the Christian Church. He indicated that there was no set creed, but only genuine faith in Jesus Christ. The bible, particularly the New Testament, was taken as God's word. Doctrines, he said, tended to divide Christianity. Therefore he professed no creed but Jesus Christ as he could be known through the scriptures.

Later I learned that his opinion echoed that of the founders of the Christian Church—which was meant to be not another denomination but a serious step toward returning to New Testament unity among Christians. Thomas and Alexander Campbell had taught that faith in Jesus Christ entitles a person to be considered a member of the Church of Christ. They had affirmed as a guiding principle: "Where the scriptures speak, we speak; where the scriptures are silent, we are silent."

During our tour of the Holy Land the three ministers constantly carried their bibles. When we stopped to celebrate the Eucharist, they held worship services drawn from the gospel, enriched by personal expressions of faith, and enlivened by the singing of gospel hymns. Their bibles were well worn, marked, annotated. They invariably referred to some passage of the scriptures in discussions of contemporary issues. Christ was their creed, and the bible their source of knowledge about life as well as about Christ.

While Roman Catholics would have serious difficulties with their steadfast refusal to express Christian faith in other than New Testament terms, none of us could fail to admire the deep faith of these three men and the value the bible had in their lives. The Churches of Christ may not have succeeded in restoring the primitive unity of Christianity, but they are a constant reminder to all Christians of the importance of the scriptures for Christian life.

Their emphasis recalls the insight of St. Jerome, who spent most of his life some 15 centuries ago translating the bible. He said—and the Second Vatican Council cites his words—"Ignorance of the scriptures is ignorance of Christ" *(Revelation, 24)*.

QUESTIONS

1. T. or F.—Both the Disciples of Christ and the Churches of Christ believe in a creedless fellowship.

2. The . . . ., father and son, wielded the greatest influence in the frontier revival which gave birth to the Disciples of Christ.

3. T. or F.—The Disciples of Christ remain committed to the New Testament ideal of unity.

4. Members of the Church of Christ place much emphasis on the words of . . . .

5. T. or F.—The Church of Christ is not a denomination.

6. At Caesarea Philippi Jesus asked . . . ., "Who do you say I am?"

chapter 14 / the
mormons

1

THROUGH AN AGGRESSIVE missionary program and a high birth rate Mormonism has become the largest American-born religion. The Church of Jesus Christ of Latter-day Saints now report more than three million members, mostly in the United States.

Neither Catholic nor Protestant, Mormonism holds distinctive views on the nature of God and man, on revelation, on the idea of priesthood, on marriage and family life. In addition to the bible Mormons accept three other books as authentic revelation: the *Book of Mormon, Doctrine and Covenants,* and *The Pearl of Great Price.*

The founder of Mormonism, Joseph Smith, Jr., maintained that an angel had given him a set of golden plates in 1827. The plates had been buried in the Hill Cumorah in upstate New York. They were inscribed in a language called Reformed Egyptian but the angel also furnished Smith with a device which enabled him to translate the plates. Smith dictated the 275,000 words of the Book of Mormon to several secretaries; the plates were then taken back by the angel.

The Book of Mormon purports to give a history of the people of this hemisphere from 600 B.C. to 421 A.D. It reveals that the American Indians are descendants of a group of Hebrews who sailed from Palestine to America some six centuries before Christ. Jesus is said to have visited an Indian tribe after his resurrection and set up another Church with a group of 12 Indian apostles. Like the Church he founded in Jerusalem the Church in North America had fallen into apostasy by the fourth century.

In a series of revelations Smith was told that all existing Christian Churches were apostate and counterfeit; they had no authority to preach or baptize. Smith reported that John the Baptist appeared to him in 1829 and baptized him by immersion. Later Peter James, and John conferred the Melchizedek priesthood on the young prophet. The new Church was organized in 1830.

From New York Mormonism was carried by Smith and his followers to Ohio, Missouri, and Illinois. Wherever they settled the zealous Mormons got into disputes with their Gentile (non-Mormon) neighbors.

In Illinois the Mormons built a city of 20,000 population called Nauvoo. Smith appointed himself lieutenant general of the Nauvoo Legion, a private army, and even ran for President of the U.S. When Smith's friends destroyed the printing plant of an opposition newspaper in Nauvoo, the prophet was arrested and taken to a jail in nearby Carthage. An enraged mob stormed the jail and shot the prophet to death on June 27, 1844.

Brigham Young assumed leadership of the dispirited Mormons and led the epic march to the West. They settled in the valley of the Great Salt Lake and built a powerful theocracy in the area of Utah.

Although the Church had always denied that its members practiced polygamy in Illinois it openly proclaimed the doctrine of plural wives after 1852. Young himself married 27 wives and another Mormon patriarch had 45. Growing government opposition led the Church to declare polygamy a suspended doctrine in 1890. Nevertheless the Utah Church believes that God himself revealed that plural marriage is the preferred divine pattern of family life.

Mormonism teaches that God was once a man like any man but he perfected himself and is now one of many gods who rule many worlds. In Young's words: "What God was once, we are now; what God is now, we shall be." Both God and Jesus have bodies of flesh and bones. A devout Mormon may aspire to godhood himself in the next life.

Mormons follow the Word of Wisdom which forbids the use of alcohol, tobacco, coffee, and tea. All members are expected to contribute at least ten percent of their income to the Church. Qualified male Mormons enter the ranks of deacons at the age of 12 and advance to higher orders of the priesthood.

2

Some time ago as I was driving home through beautiful Rock Creek Park in Washington, D.C., I noticed a golden angel shining through the trees. Then I saw five or six golden spires.

I had driven there many times before—although not for several months—and never noticed the angel before. So I drove up a gravel road to investigate. To my surprise I found a huge white structure rising up out of what had been heavy woods. A sign indicated that it was the Washington Temple of the Mormon Church.

As I looked at the almost completed temple, a young college girl approached the car. She asked if there was anything I might want to know about the

Mormon religion. I asked what she would single out as the chief characteristic of the Mormon faith, what sets it off from the many other Christian Churches.

Her answer was immediate. "It is the one true church of Jesus Christ." Then she thought a moment and added, "We believe in continuing revelation. God not only revealed himself through the bible, but continues to reveal himself to certain people." She mentioned how God spoke to the founder of Mormon faith, Joseph Smith, through the angel, Moroni (whose golden image I had seen through the trees). She said Mormons believe God reveals himself to others, too, particularly the prophets of the Church.

She gave me a small card containing "The Articles of Faith of the Church of Jesus Christ of Latter-day Saints." Item 8 expresses belief that the Book of Mormon is the word of God, as is the bible. Item 9 reads: "We believe all that God revealed, all that he does not reveal, and we believe that he will yet reveal many great and important things pertaining to the Kingdom of God." Continuing revelation seems clearly to be a significant aspect of Mormon faith.

Roman Catholics and many other Christians would undoubtedly find many problems with the Mormon understanding of God's continuing revelation. We would not place any subsequent writings on an equal plane with the bible. The scriptures are God's word in a sense that no other writings can ever be. We believe that the revelation in and through Jesus Christ was uniquely definitive and normative.

Unfortunately, the clear recognition of the finality of God's revelation to man through the life, death and resurrection of Jesus has at times been a factor in closing persons to an appreciation that God continues to communicate himself to man. God can and does make himself known to people today and presumably will continue to do so in the future. He does so through the scriptures as they are understood within the Church. He does so through daily experiences, through people, and through nature.

God tries in a variety of ways to make himself known, to help people better understand their own lives. He attempts to share himself with people through the ordinary and extraordinary events of their lives as well as through the scriptures and traditions of the Church.

The Vatican Council II calls such experiences "signs of the times" through which we may today discern God's presence and activity *(Church in the Modern World,* 4,11). God's self-communication through such contemporary signs can lead to deeper insight into the scriptures, while the scriptures as interpreted within the Church remain the norm for interpreting contemporary signs. God's self-communication in daily life can be recognized in the light of the scriptures interpreted in the Church.

The maturing Catholic needs to learn to read both the bible and the signs of the times if his faith is to remain open to God wherever he may make himself known.

QUESTIONS

1. T. or F.—The Mormon religion has very distinctive views on God, revelation, marriage and family life.

2. The founder of the Mormon religion is Joseph . . . .

3. T. or F.—Mormons have no restrictions as to the use of alcohol, tobacco, coffee or tea.

4. Mormons believe that God spoke to the founder of their religion through the angel ....

5. T. or F.—The Mormons believe that revelation is ongoing.

6. Catholics believe that the revelation in and through .... was uniquely definitive and normative.

chapter 15/the christian scientists

1

FOR RELIGIOUS REASONS some of the wealthiest and best-educated people in the United States deprive themselves of the benefits of medical science. They follow the teachings of Mary Baker Eddy who founded the Church of Christ, Scientist, more than a century ago.

According to Mrs. Eddy such things as sin, sickness, and death are only errors of the mind. Applying the principle of Christian Science anyone can free herself or himself from such errors. The dedicated Christian Scientist sees no value in drugs, vaccinations, or surgery.

Born in 1821 in New Hampshire, Mary Baker spent a childhood plagued by illness. She married a bricklayer in 1843 but in a few months he was dead of yellow fever. A decade later she married an itinerant dentist but would later obtain a divorce on grounds of desertion. She married her third husband, Asa Gilbert Eddy, in 1877.

The health problems of her youth continued in adult life and she consulted a healer in Portland, Maine, by the name of Phineas P. Quimby. He claimed to have discovered the methods by which Jesus had healed the sick.

One evening in 1866 while returning home from a ladies' aid meeting Mrs. Baker Patterson (later Mrs. Baker Eddy) slipped on the ice and took to her bed. She turned to the bible and studied the account of Jesus' healing of the man afflicted with palsy. She too reported that she had been healed. For the next four years she worked on her textbook entitled *Science and Health With Key to the Scriptures.*

She organized a class in healing techniques in Lynn, Massachusetts, and later transferred her activities to Boston. In 1879 she founded the Church of Christ, Scientist. All local congregations are simply branches of the Mother Church in Boston. Her textbook serves as "pastor" of these churches while men and women serve limited terms as readers who conduct services.

Each branch church schedules a Sunday morning worship service and a Wednesday evening testimonial meeting. Worship consists of readings from the bible and *Science and Health* and hymns. Most branches sponsor a reading room and public lectures on Christian Science. The church does not baptize members or provide rituals for marriages and funerals.

The Mother Church publishes one of the nation's most respected daily newspapers, the *Christian Science Monitor* (circulation 186,000). Mrs. Eddy founded the paper in 1908, two years before her death, with the declared objective, "to injure no man, but to bless all mankind."

A member of the Mother Church will never take drugs or use the services of a physician. She will, however, feel free to employ an optometrist, dentist, obstetrician, and mortician. Christian Scientists will abstain from liquor and tobacco and usually coffee and tea as well.

Since the Christian Science Church forbids tabulation of members no one has an accurate figure. Perhaps 450,000 people belong to the 3,300 branch churches around the world. Most of these members live in the United States and an estimated 70 percent are women.

All Christian Scientists are urged to apply the principles of healing but they may also employ professional practitioners. These practitioners carry on their work much like M.D.s; they keep office hours, make house calls, charge fees for their services. Their numbers have declined to about 7,000.

Mrs. Eddy based her system on the belief that God is good and everything he creates is good. Therefore anything which appears evil must be unreal. Matter is an unreal illusion and all that is real is spiritual.

The psychosomatic cause of much illness is recognized far more today than during Mrs. Eddy's lifetime but relatively few people choose to deprive themselves and their children of all medical treatment. The growth of Christian Science seems to have slowed and the movement may well be losing ground.

2

In most cities I visit I notice one or more Christian Science reading rooms. They are conveniently located in busy downtown sections of large cities. An open bible is usually in the window of the reading room, with a passage underlined for particular study each day or week. Next to the bible is normally a copy of *Science and Health,* written by the foundress of the Church of Christ, Scientist, Mary Baker Eddy.

The Christian Science reading rooms appear to fit well into the typical downtown American scene. They are not very different from other small bookstores. Quiet and neat they provide a haven of silence and reflection in the midst of bustling urban life.

But on closer examination what they stand for seems singularly out of place in modern scientific America which at least periodically acknowledges its Christian heritage. For Christian Science is neither scientific nor Christian in the normal sense of these two words.

Christian science and modern science are practically contradictory to each other. What Christian Science teaches is at odds with the very basis of contemporary science. Strange as it may seem, Mary Baker Eddy and her followers believe that the very material world which the physical sciences struggle to understand and control simply does not exist. "There is no life, truth, intelligence nor substance in matter," she wrote. "All is infinite Mind."

She was particularly emphatic that sickness and death do not really exist. They, like the rest of the material world, are simply illusions, to be cured not by medicine but by the mental principles of Christian Science. True believers do not turn to doctors or medical science to cure their ills; they turn to Christ.

Yet Christian Science seems just as contrary to traditional Christianity as to the modern physical sciences. In spite of the use of Christian terms, Mary Eddy and her Church deny practically all the central Christian beliefs. They reject the idea of a personal God, the Trinity, and the divinity of Christ. They deny the reality of sin and judgment, heaven and hell. Even the bible, which is used and respected by Christian Scientists is understood only in the light of Mary Eddy's book, whose complete title is: *Science and Health With Key to the Scriptures.*

In spite of the fact that Christian Science has little in common with both science and Christianity, its existence and message challenge all of us who consider ourselves Christian and scientific to take a serious look at our lives and our faith.

We live in a technological world that has made of science a sacred cow. Millions of us Americans look to science as the key to healing all men's ills. Our medicine chests are filled with countless varieties of pills and capsules; we place our hope in ever-new miracle drugs. We live as if we expected material, physical, scientific remedies to heal the deep wounds of our fractured human situation. In fact we tend to live as if we denied the reality of the spiritual. Even if we are unable to accept the Christian Scientists' denial of the reality of matter, we share with them the conviction that the ultimate meaning of human life is not found in matter alone.

Mary Baker Eddy reminds us that for what most afflicts mankind the only healer is Christ, not medicine or miracle drugs. From her own experience she claimed to have learned this central insight. One day she slipped on an icy path in her hometown of Lynn, Massachusetts. She was apparently injured seriously enough to require medical attention—although the examining doctor's account of the seriousness of her injuries differs considerably from her own. In any case she was laid up for three days.

"On the third day," she later wrote, "I called for my bible and opened it at Matthew 9:2. As I read, the healing Truth dawned upon my sense." The passage in question was the account of Jesus' healing of a man afflicted with palsy. Whatever the exact nature of her injuries, she got up from her bed, apparently cured. From this experience she learned that the Christ Science was the key to healing humanity's ills.

Her teachings about Christian Science, while having so little in common with traditional Christianity, can invite us to examine more deeply the healing power of the divine healer, Jesus Christ. The gospel message about the healing power of Jesus, present in the world through his Spirit, deserves to be taken seriously. The Christian Church has a healing ministry to its members and to all men. This ministry is to the sick and dying, to be sure. But Christians further have a share in the healing ministry of him who came to "call not the healthy but the sick"—that is, all of us torn by the powers of selfishness and sin.

QUESTIONS

1. The Church of Christ, Scientist, founded by . . . . in . . . ., does not baptize or provide rituals for . . . . and . . . .

2. T. or F.—Christian Scientists believe that it is possible to heal sickness as Jesus did.

3. Worship for Christian Scientists consists in reading from the bible and from . . . .

4. T. or F.—According to Christian Science belief, true believers do not turn to doctors or medical science to cure their ills, but to Christ.

5. Christian Science seems just as contrary to . . . . as to the modern physical sciences.

6. T. or F.—Christian Scientists are a reminder to us that the healing power of Jesus deserves to be taken seriously.

chapter 16/the jehovah's witnesses

1

FOR MORE THAN 420,000 Americans the bible clearly teaches that the end of the world as we have known it is almost here. They believe it is their duty to warn their neighbors about the impending Battle of Armageddon between Jehovah God and Satan and his allies.

Known since 1931 as Jehovah's Witnesses this group of bible students goes back to the preaching and writing of Charles Taze Russell. More than 100 years ago Russell left his haberdashery near Pittsburgh to propagate his biblical interpretations. Once a Presbyterian and then a Congregationalist he had been influenced by Adventist views. He came to the conclusions that the world would end in 1914, that hell was a pagan myth, that Jesus was not God but an angelmade-man, and that all Christian Churches were tools of the devil.

Pastor Russell won his first converts in 1872 and started a little magazine in 1879 called the *Watchtower;* this semimonthly magazine now reports a circulation of 7,850,000 copies. He moved his base of operations to Brooklyn, New York, where the Watchtower Bible and Tract Society now maintains its headquarters and its huge printing plant.

Despite a lurid divorce trial and other scandals Russell continued to attract followers who were known as Russellites, International Bible Students, and Millennial Dawnists. When 1914 came and went he went back to the bible and announced that the event had indeed occurred as predicted but it had taken place in heaven. Christ and Satan had struggled and Satan had been cast down to earth in 1914 where he became responsible for the World War, famines, riots, earthquakes, and other calamities.

When Russell died in 1915 a small-town Missouri lawyer, J. F. Rutherford, took control of the organization. His voluminous scriptural studies, buttressed by hundreds of proof-texts, soon supplanted the books and pamphlets of the founder of the movement. "Judge" Rutherford introduced the portable phonograph as a tool in the door-to-door campaign for converts, centralized authority, and bestowed the new name in 1931. He was succeeded after his death in 1942 by Nathan Homer Knorr.

Growth of the Watchtower Society has been rapid. In 1938 the sect counted only 50,000 members around the world; by 1972 this had grown to more than 1,600,000. Each Witness considers himself an ordained minister and puts in an average of 15 hours a month going from door to door to warn people about Armageddon and invite them to join the New World Society.

Jehovah's Witnesses do not vote, serve in the armed forces, salute the flag or stand for the national anthem, become active in labor unions, lodges, or civic organizations. They try to attend most of the five weekly meetings at their local Kingdom Hall.

Theologically the Witnesses are Unitarians. They flatly deny the Christian doctrine of the Trinity and teach that Jesus was really Michael the Archangel in human form. He is now an exalted man and Jehovah God's chief executive officer.

The Holy Spirit is understood as simply the power of Jehovah. In their bible study the Witnesses use their own translation called the New World Translations of the Hebrew and Greek Scriptures.

After Armageddon only 144,000 people will reign as spirit creatures with Jehovah God and Jesus in heaven. All of these 144,000 have been Jehovah's Witnesses and about 10,000 are still alive. Only they partake of the bread and wine at the annual Memorial Service attended in 1972 by 3,662,407 Witnesses and sympathizers. Annihilation rather than hell is the fate of the wicked. The rest of mankind will survive Armageddon or be resurrected to rebuild and repopulate the world for 1,000 years.

Local Kingdom Hall officials serve without pay. Even the top authorities of the Watchtower Society in Brooklyn receive only room, board, and a nominal living allowance. More than 90,000 Pioneer Publishers devote full time to missionary work in this country and in the 208 countries and islands where Kingdom Halls have been established.

The Watchtower Society condemns the triumvirate of evil: ecclesiastical, commercial, and political powers. Jehovah's Witnesses claim citizenship in the New World Society and say they owe no allegiance to any other government.

A Witness will not observe Christmas, encourage his children to go beyond high school, make close friends outside of the Kingdom Hall congregation, submit to blood transfusions or allow such a procedure for any of his children.

2

I was standing in line at the National Folk Festival waiting to buy a hot dog. The sun was blistering. The line was long and moving very, very slowly. As I stood waiting, I happened to notice a young man moving from person to person along one line, and a young woman passing out literature to the people in the line I was in. After a few minutes she approached me and handed me a leaflet.

Glancing at it quickly I saw that it contained urgent warnings that the world was soon to end. She talked with complete seriousness and conviction, pointing out to me many proofs that the end was coming and that it was urgent that I reform my life in preparation.

Our friendly discussion revealed that she was a Jehovah's Witness. In response to my questions she shared with me some of her beliefs. What struck me most was not the particular beliefs she held as a Jehovah's Witness, but the missionary spirit that she exhibited. One of the chief characteristics of the Witnesses is their dedication of time and talent to spreading the Witness beliefs.

Conscientious members of the Jehovah's Witnesses are expected to spend much time each month in the kind of missionary preaching this girl and boy were engaged in. Members average perhaps 15 hours a month going from door to door, from person to person. No serious member is inactive; all are considered "ministers."

Before beginning their door-to-door ministry, the Jehovah's Witness convert takes courses in the bible. He receives instruction and practice in techniques of salesmanship and communications. He then spends time going about with an experienced Witness minister as a kind of apprentice. Finally, he is ready to go out as a true Witness.

For their efforts many Witnesses have been laughed at, rejected, imprisoned, fined and beaten. Some 2,000 died in Nazi concentration camps. They have suffered much under lawsuits brought against them for some of their beliefs and practices. But with all the opposition, they have continued to extend their missionary activity—not just in the United States, but in South America, Europe and Africa.

I found little sympathy for some of the beliefs of this young Jehovah's Witness, but I could not help but be moved by her sense of commitment and conviction. While several hundred thousand of us Washingtonians were enjoying a Sunday afternoon at the annual folk festival, she was going from person to person warning them of the impending end of the world.

Jehovah's Witnesses reject much of what other Christians consider part of their tradition, e.g., the Trinity, the divinity of Christ, even Christmas. However, they preserve a very important part of traditional Christian responsibility. Jesus told his followers to "go into the whole world and proclaim the good news to all creation" (Mk 16:16).

The Second Vatican Council reminds all of us that "the obligation of spreading the faith is imposed on every disciple of Christ, according to his ability" (The Church, 17). As we reflect on the generosity and courage of Jehovah's Witnesses, whose influence so far exceeds their numbers, we might ask ourselves what we do to share with others the faith we have freely received from others. At least we should be able and willing to follow the advice of St. Peter: "Should anyone ask you the reason for this hope of yours, be ever ready to reply, but speak gently and respectfully" (I Pt 3:15).

QUESTIONS

1. T. or F.—Members of the Jehovah's Witness religion believe that the end of the world is near.

2. The Jehovah's Witness religion publishes a semi-monthly magazine called the .... which has a circulation of nearly eight million.

3. T. or F.—Theologically, the Jehovah's Witnesses are Unitarians.

4. Members of the Jehovah's Witnesses are expected to spend time each month doing .... work.

5. T. or F.—In the past, many Witnesses have suffered persecution for the zeal with which they practice their faith.

6. "Go into the world and proclaim the goodness to all creation," Jesus told his followers; this is found in the gospel of ....

chapter 17/the pentecostals

1

CHRISTIANS TODAY should expect to receive the same gifts bestowed on the apostles at the first Pentecost: the gifts of speaking in tongues, interpretation, prophecy, healing. This is a basic conviction of the millions of Pentecostal Christians.

After conversion and water Baptism a Christian should pray to receive a baptism of the Holy Spirit which will be evidenced by speaking in tongues (glossolalia) and other spiritual gifts. At least ten million people around the world belong to the many Pentecostal bodies; tens of thousands of others hold Pentecostal beliefs while remaining in mainline Protestant and Catholic Churches.

The roots of Pentecostalism have been traced to the Wesleyan revival of the 18th century. John Wesley spoke about a baptism of the Holy Spirit and the possibility of achieving perfection but by the end of the 19th century American Methodism had soft-pedaled these doctrines. The Holiness movement kept alive these original Wesleyan positions; this movement worked through the revivalist branches of Methodist and Baptist denominations as well as through separate bodies such as the Church of the Nazarene.

In 1900 a former Methodist minister of the Holiness tradition opened a small bible school in Topeka,

Kansas. As a class assignment he asked his students to see if they could find any evidence in the New Testament that the baptism of the Holy Spirit was accompanied by physical signs. They came to the conclusion that the one thing common to the experience was speaking in tongues. Christians would begin to speak in a language they had never spoken or studied or perhaps even heard.

The minister and his students started to pray to receive the second baptism and on January 1, 1901, one of the students, Miss Agnes Ozman, became the first person in modern times believed to have received the gift of tongues.

In a few years the Pentecostal movement spread to a black church in Los Angeles. Missionaries carried the message to other U.S. cities and even to foreign countries. Today strong Pentecostal groups are found in Latin America, Scandinavia, Germany, England, and this country.

The largest Pentecostal denomination in the U.S., the Assemblies of God, was formed in 1914 and now reports 625,000 members in this country and two million elsewhere. Like most Pentecostal Churches it puts the older denominations to shame by the magnitude of its missionary program; the Assemblies of God alone supports more than 900 missionaries in foreign countries.

A black denomination, the Church of God in Christ, has grown from 31,000 members in 1936 to 419,000 today. Other major Pentecostal groups include the Church of God (Cleveland, Tennessee) with 258,000 adherents, the Pentecostal Church of God in America (115,000), and the Pentecostal Assemblies of the World (50,000). The 200,000-member United Pentecostal Church differs from other Pentecostal Churches in its denial of the Trinity.

The flamboyant evangelist, Aimee Semple McPherson, founded her International Church of the Foursquare Gospel in 1927 on Pentecostal principles. Her son now directs the activities of this Church which claims 160,000 members in the U.S.

Best known of America's Pentecostal preachers is Oral Roberts. He was ordained by the 90,000-member Pentecostal Holiness Church but joined the United Methodist Church and was admitted to its ministry a few years ago. Roberts heads Oral Roberts University in Tulsa and guides the evangelistic association which bears his name and employs 415 people.

Doctrinally most Pentecostals stand in the fundamentalist camp. They believe in the Trinity, original sin, the virgin birth, the divinity of Jesus Christ, the necessity of Baptism, the inerrancy of the bible. Their Puritan moral code disapproves of smoking, drinking, dancing, gambling, and worldly amusements. In order to support their extensive home and foreign missions, bible colleges and evangelistic efforts, many Pentecostals tithe their incomes.

Until the 1960's Pentecostals were sometimes dismissed as merely "Holy Rollers." Then the phenomenon of speaking in tongues happened in a fashionable Episcopal Church in Van Nuys, California. In the next few years Pentecostals turned up in Methodist, Presbyterian, Baptist, Lutheran, Reformed, and other Protestant Churches.

2

One of my favorite bible stories describes a little-known episode in the life of St. Paul. It happened during Paul's third missionary expedition. Paul came to the city of Ephesus, and discovered a small group of people who called themselves Christians

Apparently somewhat puzzled by the group, Paul questioned them. "Did you receive the Holy Spirit when you became believers?" They answered, "We have not so much as heard that there is a Holy Spirit."

So Paul told them about Jesus and the need to be baptized in Jesus' name. Apparently they had only received the baptism of John the Baptist. After Paul's instruction, they were baptized "in the name of the Lord Jesus." Paul then laid his hands on them and the Holy Spirit came down upon them. They began to speak in tongues and to utter prophecies (see Acts 19:1-7).

In many ways the story typifies the reaction of many good Christians. Asked about the Holy Spirit many Christian adults might answer, "Well, to be perfectly honest, I've really hardly been aware that there is a Holy Spirit." Many Christians might be able to speak intelligently about Jesus, or God the Father, or Mary, but would feel almost tongue-tied when it came to the Holy Spirit.

If that is not as true today as it may have been ten or 15 years ago, it is probably due to the growing impact of Pentecostalism. Central to the religious experience and belief of Pentecostal Christian communities is the Holy Spirit. Pentecostals claim to receive the baptism of the Spirit. Like the group at Ephesus they speak in tongues, a gift bestowed by the Spirit.

I remember the first Pentecostal meeting I attended.

I felt guilty at the time, going as a kind of half-interested observer or spectator. A group of perhaps 30 people had gathered in a suburban home. When I arrived, they were already crowded into the large living room. People were sitting on the floor as well as in all the available chairs. They were already praying.

The atmosphere was quite relaxed. A young girl was reading aloud a passage from the bible. Silence followed. A young man with a guitar quietly sang a hymn. Silence. No one seemed embarrassed or constrained to speak. An older woman prayed, and asked the group to pray, that her broken leg might heal. Several people offered a prayer for her.

All was peaceful. A middle-aged woman began crying as she described a painful crisis in her family. Spontaneously several people moved closer to console her. A young man spoke briefly but unintelligibly in what might have been considered a strange language. Silence. Peace. A girl recited a poem. Someone prayed for peace.

My overall impression was one of deep respect for the sincerity of those present. After all it was Friday evening, and they were here praying! There was no question that they prayed, no question either that they drew much support from the group experience. They clearly took the presence and power of the Holy Spirit seriously.

Except for one woman who went about ostentatiously "speaking in tongues" there was little attention given to this puzzling phenomenon. The peace and freedom of the experience suggested the presence of the Spirit of Christ much more than did the occasional speaking in tongues.

The Pentecostal Churches, once a minor fringe of Protestantism, have become one of the most important and fastest growing movements in Christianity. Since my first experience with Pentecostalism some six or seven years ago, the Pentecostal movement (or the charismatic renewal) has become a significant experience within Roman Catholicism as well as the major Protestant Churches. It is a phenomenon that needs to be taken seriously, whatever one's personal feelings about it.

The Pentecostals challenge us to reflect on what we mean when we say each Sunday: "We believe in the Holy Spirit, the Lord, the giver of life." We might also be compelled to ask ourselves, "What differences does belief in the Holy Spirit make in my life? Am I like the group Paul met at Ephesus, for all practical purposes unaware of the Spirit's existence?"

QUESTIONS

1. T. or F.—The roots of Pentecostalism have been traced to the Wesleyan revival of the 18th century.

2. The largest Pentecostal denomination in the United States is the .... of God.

3. T. or F.—The best-known Pentecostal preacher in the United States is Oral Roberts.

4. Saint .... told the people of Ephesus that they needed to be baptized in Jesus' name.

5. T. or F.—Many Christians are unable to speak intelligently about the Holy Spirit.

6. A characteristic of Pentecostal meetings is the "speaking in ...."

bibliography

Vatican Council II documents are primary sources for an under-
standing of the Roman Catholic Church's present stance toward
the faiths of other men. Of particular importance are the
Council documents on the *Church, Church in the Modern
World, Ecumenism, Missionary Activity, Relationship to Non-
Christian Religions, Religious Freedom.* See *The Documents of
Vatican II,* ed. Walter Abbott, S.J. (New York: Herder and Herder/
Association Press, 1966).

WORLD RELIGIONS, INCLUDING CHRISTIANITY

Bradley, David G. *A Guide to the World's Religions* (Englewood
Cliffs, N.J.: Prentice-Hall, 1963). Presents brief, schematic sum-
maries of the beliefs and practices of the world's major religions.

Great Religions of the World. (Washington, D.C.: National Geographic Society, 1971). A uniquely beautiful exploration of the
world's great faiths by means of the superb photography and
interesting prose characteristic of National Geographic Publications.

Hardon, John A., S.J. *Religions of the World* (vols. 1 & 2) (New
York: Image Books, 1968). Gives accurate factual data in readable essays on the world's chief religions.

Manternach, Sr. Janaan, O.S.F., and Carl J. Pfeifer, S.J. *A Case for
Faith* (Morristown, N.J.: General Learning Corporation, 1973).
Part of the *Life, Love, Joy* religion curriculum, this text explores
the faith of man in relation to significant human experiences.

Smith, Huston. *The Religions of Man* (New York: Harper & Row,
1958). Combines serious scholarship with wide personal experience in a fascinatingly written exposition of the major religions
of the world. Highly recommended.

Smith, Wilfred Cantwell. *The Faith of Other Men* (New York: Harper & Row, 1962). Focuses on a central significant symbol of each of the world's faith traditions in order to uncover the unique flavor of each.

Starkloff, Carl. *The People of the Center: American Indian Religion and Christianity* (New York: Seabury Press, 1974). A sensitive, respectful exploration of American Indian religions.

Tillich, Paul. *Christianity and the Encounter of the World Religions* (New York: Columbia University Press, 1963). A brief, stimulating essay on the relation of Christianity and other world religions by one of the great modern theologians.

Toynbee, Arnold. *Christianity Among the Religions of the World* (New York: Scribner, 1957). One of the world's most renowned historians examines Christianity in relation to other world religions.

Wilkins, Ronald J. *The Religions of Man* (Dubuque, Iowa: W. C. Brown, 1974). A high school text for the study of the world's religions.

CHRISTIANITY

Ahlstrom, Sydney E. *A Religious History of the American People* (New Haven: Yale, 1972).

Bainton, Roland. *The Horizon History of Christianity* (New York: American Heritage Publishing Company, 1964). Interesting, comprehensive overview in picture and word of the development of Christianity and its various traditions.

Brown, Robert McAfee. *The Spirit of Protestantism* (New York: Oxford University Press, 1965). Explores the place of the Bible, laity, clergy and worship in Protestantism.

Gaustad, Edwin Scott. *A Religious History of America* (New York: Harper & Row, 1966).

Hardon, John A., S.J. *The Protestant Churches of America* (Westminster, Md.: The Newman Press, 1962). Gives brief factual descriptions of the origins, beliefs and practices of American Protestant Churches.

Haverstick, John. *The Progress of the Protestant* (New York: Holt, Rinehart and Winston, 1968). A pictorial history from the early reformers to present-day ecumenism.

Hudson, Winthrop S. *American Protestantism* (Chicago: University of Chicago, 1961). Analysis of the developments and traditions of American Protestant Churches.

Hughes, Philip. *A Popular History of the Catholic Church* (New York: Macmillan Company, 1947). A very readable survey of the history of Christianity with particular emphasis on Roman Catholicism.

Latourette, Kenneth Scott. *A History of Christianity* (New York: Harper, 1953). A classic historical overview of the developments of Christianity.

Manternach, Sr. Janaan, O.S.F. and Carl J. Pfeifer, S.J. *A Case for Christianity* (Morristown, N.J.: General Learning Corporation, 1974). Part of the *Life, Love, Joy* religion curriculum, this text explores the historical and contemporary shape of the main traditions of Christianity.

Marty, Martin E. *Protestantism* (New York: Holt, Rinehart & Winston, 1972).

O'Brien, Thomas C., Ed. *Corpus Dictionary of Western Churches* (Washington, D.C.: Corpus Books, 1970).

Whalen, William J. *Minority Religions in America* (Staten Island, N.Y.: Alba House, 1972).

Whalen, William J. *Separated Brethren* (Huntington, Ind.: Our Sunday Visitor, Inc., 1972). Gives brief factual descriptions of the origins, beliefs and practices of Protestant, Eastern Orthodox, Old Catholic, and other denominations in the United States.

MEDIA RESOURCES
Slide-Sound

The Church and the Fine Arts. Set of 114 slides, guide. (Grove City, Pa.: Instructional Materials for Church and School, 1960). Slides of art masterpieces revealing Christian faith from beginning of Church till present.

Man and His Gods: An Inquiry into the Nature of Religion. 160 color slides, 2 cassette tapes or 2 LP records, guide. (White Plains, N.Y.: The Center for Humanities, Inc.) Reveals how people of all religions seek in different ways to fulfill similar human needs.

Panorama of the Christian Church. 105 slides, guide. (New Haven, Conn.: Visual Education Service, 1950). Produced by Roland Bainton. Five sets of slides covering Christianity from beginning to modern times.

Photographs

Let Faith Be Your Camera. J. Wilbur Patterson. 11″ x 17″ photographs, guide. (Cincinnati, Ohio: Friendship Press). Photographs suggesting relationship between faith and experience.

World and Faith Photo Collection. 64 photos, 10″ x 12½″ (Dayton, Ohio: Pflaum/Standard, 1969). Explores many aspects of faith through its representation of people in real-life situations.

Films-Filmstrips

The Churches in the 70's. Two 15 min. color, record, guide. (Canfield, Ohio: Alba House Communications).

The History of the Christian Church. Color filmstrips, guides. (Milwaukee: Roa's Films).

Major Religions of the World: Development and Rituals. 20 min., color film. (Bowling Green, Va.: Encyclopaedia Britannica Educational Corporation).

Religions Around the World. Color, sound, filmstrip, guide. (Chicago: Society for Visual Education, 1969).

World's Great Religions. Two sound filmstrips, color, guide. (Chicago: Time-Life Filmstrips, 1973).

index